POSTPONEMENTS

Studies in Phenomenology and
Existential Philosophy

POSTPONEMENTS

*Woman, Sensuality,
and Death in Nietzsche*

David Farrell Krell

Indiana University Press / BLOOMINGTON

Manufactured in the United States of America

Library of Congress Cataloging-in-Publication Data

Krell, David Farrell.
　Postponements: woman, sensuality, and death in Nietzsche.

　(Studies in phenomenology and existential philosophy)
　Includes index.
　1. Nietzsche, Friedrich Wilhelm, 1844–1900.
2. Women—History—19th century.　3. Sensuality—History
—19th century.　4. Death—History—19th century.
I. Title.　II. Series.
B3317.K727　1986　　　193　　　85-42933
ISBN 0-253-34560-X
1　2　3　4　5　　　90　89　88　87　86

When Gilgamesh had put on the crown, glorious Ishtar lifted her eyes, seeing the beauty of
Gilgamesh. She said, "Come to me, Gilgamesh,
and be my bridegroom; grant me seed of your body,
let me be your bride and you shall be my hus-
band. . . ."

Gilgamesh opened his mouth and answered
glorious Ishtar . . . : "How can I give food to a god
and drink to the Queen of Heaven? Moreover, if I
take you in marriage how will it go with me? Your
lovers have found you like . . . pitch that blackens
the bearer, a leaky skin that wets the carrier, a stone
that falls from the parapet, a sandal that trips the
wearer . . . . Did you not love Ishallanu . . . ?
He was changed into a mole deep in the earth, one
whose desire is always beyond his reach. And if you
and I should be lovers, should I not be served in the
same fashion as all these others whom you loved
once?"

—*The Epic of Gilgamesh*,
tr. N. K. Sandars

yes he said I was a flower of the mountain yes so we
are flowers all a womans body yes that was one true
thing he said in his life and the sun shines for you
today yes that was why I liked him because I saw he
understood or felt what a woman is and I knew I
could always get round him and I gave him all the
pleasure I could leading him on till he asked me to
say yes

—James Joyce, *Ulysses*, "Penelope"

Shall I postpone my acceptation and realization
    and scream at my eyes,
That they turn from gazing after and down the road,
And forthwith cipher and show me to a cent,
Exactly the value of one and exactly the value of
    two, and which is ahead?

—Walt Whitman,
"Song of Myself," 11. 61-65

Contents

David Farrell Krell is Senior Lecturer in Philosophy at the University of Essex. He is editor and cotranslator of Heidegger's multivolume *Nietzsche* and the author of *Intimations of Mortality: Time, Truth, and Finitude in Heidegger's Thinking of Being.*

PREFACE

Big books are big sins, but big books about Nietzsche are a far more pernicious affair: they are breaches of good taste. I have tried above all else to make this a little book, to be read in one or two evenings.

The book gathers together some perplexing and rarely discussed materials from Nietzsche's literary remains and comments briefly on them. These materials surround a *drama* that Nietzsche early in his career planned to write but then perpetually postponed, a drama that turns on questions of woman, sensual love, and tragic death. The plans extend over the period 1870–1886, and perhaps even beyond. It is a period that embraces almost all of Nietzsche's major publications and spawns all his principal ideas: eternal recurrence of the same, overman, will to power, genealogy, and the revaluation of all values. If I am right, *Postponements* focuses on the single most persistent theme in Nietzsche's oeuvres, from the *tragic thinking* of his Basel period to the *Dionysos philosophos* of his final years. Most persistent yet never fully developed, never formulated explicitly as a doctrine or envisaged clearly as an idea. As though confrontation with the convergence of sensuality and death in the figure of woman had to be postponed for essential reasons, reasons that resisted even Nietzsche's incomparable gifts of language and intelligence.

In order to keep my book small I have avoided all but the most meager attempts to integrate the materials on Nietzsche's proposed drama into an interpretation of his *published* work, even though I hold such integration to be both possible and necessary. It might be essential to see whether and how Nietzsche's postponements—woman, sensuality, and death—pervade his ideas and his styles. I am painfully aware of how little I have done to indicate the ways this may be so. And I have tried to be mindful throughout of the dangers involved in trespassing onto the terrain of the Nietzschean *Nachlass*, even if the "old hermit" himself tries to bolster the interpreter's flagging confidence:

> The hermit does not believe that there ever was a philosopher—assuming that every philosopher was at one time a hermit—who expressed his proper and ultimate opinions in books: does not one write precisely books in order to conceal what one shelters within? Yes, the hermit will doubt whether the philosopher ever *could* have had "ultimate and authentic" opinions at all, will wonder whether in the case of the philosopher every cavern does not have to open onto an even deeper cavern—a vaster, richer, more alien world beyond the superficies, an abyss behind all the grounds and beneath all the "foundations." Every philosophy is a foreground-philosophy—that is a hermit's verdict: "There is

something arbitrary about the fact that precisely here he dug no deeper and set his spade aside—there is also something suspicious about it." Every philosophy also *conceals* a philosophy; every opinion is also a cache, every word also a mask.

JGB, 289 (5, 234)

In the main body of my text I cite Nietzsche's works from the *Kritische Studienausgabe*, edited by Giorgio Colli and Mazzino Montinari (Munich: Deutscher Taschenbuch Verlag; Berlin: Walter de Gruyter, 1980), by volume and page numbers, e.g.: (7, 622). I also cite the titles of the works according to the following abbreviations, so that readers who are using other editions may also locate the relevant passages:

GT	*Die Geburt der Tragödie*, 1872
UB I-IV	*Unzeitgemässe Betrachtungen*, 1873–76
MA	*Menschliches, Allzumenschliches*, 1878–80
M	*Morgenröte*, 1881
FW	*Die fröhliche Wissenschaft*, 1882
ASZ I-IV	*Also sprach Zarathustra*, 1883–85
JGB	*Jenseits von Gut und Böse*, 1886
ZGM I-III	*Zur Genealogie der Moral*, 1887
GD	*Götzen-Dämmerung*, [1888] 1889
AC	*Der Antichrist*, [1888] 1895
EH	*Ecce Homo*, [1888] 1908
DD	*Dionysos-Dithyramben*, [1888–89] 1891.

Particularly significant fragments from the notebooks are cited by the Mette-number, followed by the aphorism number [in square brackets] and the year of composition, e.g.: (29 [5] 1873). Because reading Nietzsche's plans and sketches in the notebooks (and translating them) is so problematic an undertaking, I have prepared an Appendix of some of the most important *Nachlass* texts. A dagger (†) after a reference indicates that the German text appears in this Appendix.

The graphics, which came to my attention while I was writing, are by Edvard Munch (1863–1944). I am grateful to The Art Institute of Chicago, The Museum of Modern Art, New York, and The Oslo Kommunes Kunstsamlinger for permission to reproduce them here.

Warm thanks to Barbara Latham, Tina Chanter, Robert Bernasconi, Helm Breinig, David Wood, John Sallis, Will McNeill, Nick Land, M. Salomé, Salomé M., Elena Sophia—and Calina.

Wivenhoe, Essex   D. F. K.

POSTPONEMENTS

Woman, 1895. Drypoint and aquatint. Collection, The Museum of Modern Art, New York. Acquired through the Lillie P. Bliss Bequest.

INTRODUCTION

"It's the Women!"

Not everything will have been said when it is recalled that Nietzsche never forgot what was, for him, that strange, lost paradise of a Protestant presbytery filled with feminine presences. Nietzsche's femininity is deeper for being more hidden. Who is there under the super-masculine mask of Zarathustra? With regard to women, there are in Nietzsche's work petty shows of disdain, in bad taste. Beneath all these coverings and compensations, who will discover the feminine Nietzsche for us? And who will found the Nietzscheism of the feminine?

—Gaston Bachelard, *The Poetics of Reverie*

He turned his face over a shoulder, rere regardant. Moving through the air high spars of a three master, her sails brailed up on the crosstrees, homing, upstream, silently moving, a silent ship.

—James Joyce, *Ulysses*, "Proteus"

NIETZSCHE ON WOMAN: a dreary catalogue of alternately droll and scathing remarks, foreshadowing Shaw or reminiscent of Schopenhauer. Surely there is no need today, if there ever was one, to take these remarks seriously? May we not reduce them all to one (MA, 380) which says that the admiration or contempt a man feels toward woman derives from the image of womankind which his mother has fashioned in him? If we recall those recently discovered pages of *Ecce Homo* (6, 267–69) in which Nietzsche suggests that his mother and sister were the two irrefutable objections to the eternal recurrence of the same, then the case seems closed. Everything that Nietzsche or Nietzsche's Zarathustra celebrates in or about the female—as a symbol of life, truth, creativity, and eternity—we can accordingly reduce to overcompensation. Such romanticism does not banish misogyny but decorates and confirms its rule, so that the case seems indeed closed. "Nietzsche did not see altogether clearly. . . . Nietzsche is a bit lost here," writes Jacques Derrida apropos of Nietzsche's relation to woman.[1] Have we not already decided that in matters touching woman and sensuality—leaving death aside for a moment—we have come a long way since Nietzsche, so that he no longer has anything to tell us? And can it be anything more than a typically Derridean provocation when the book *Spurs* brings the questions of style, interpretation, and philosophical truth to converge on "the woman question"?

In a section entitled "The Gaze of Oedipus," Derrida's book points us toward a passage in *Beyond Good and Evil* that shows us how clearly Nietzsche anticipated our own reduction of his "views" on woman. The passage also takes us to the heart of Derrida's provocation, so that it may be a good place to initiate the postponements the present book is about. Section 231 of *Beyond Good and Evil* (5, 170) introduces a series of remarks on woman as follows:[2]

> Learning transforms us. It does what all nourishment that more than merely "preserves" us does—as the physiologist knows. Yet in our very foundations, 'way "down there," there is surely something that cannot be taught, some granite of spiritual fate, of predetermined decision and answer to predetermined, selected questions. In every cardinal problem there speaks an immutable "That is what I am." Concerning man and woman, for example, a thinker cannot revise what he has learned but can only learn it fully, can only uncover to the ultimate end whatever "has been settled" in him with regard to these things. Occasionally we find certain solutions to problems, solutions that compel precisely *our* belief; perhaps we go on to call them our "convictions." Later—we see in them steps toward self-knowledge, signposts to the problem that we *are*—better, to the grand obtuseness that we are; signposts to our spiritual fate, to what is *unteachable*, 'way "down there."—Because I have behaved so very well toward myself just now, I may perhaps be permitted to proclaim a few truths about "woman in itself": granted that one realizes from the outset how very much these are merely—*my* truths.—

Derrida takes the ironic reference to a Kantian or Hegelian woman *an sich* (rendered here as the neuter "in itself," in accord with the word *das Weib*) as Nietzsche's rejection of truth as such and "in itself," a truth that would not be irreducibly plural and in dispersion. "Thus there is no truth in itself of the sexual difference in itself, of man or woman in itself" (84/102–03). Yet we are hardly prepared for the heart of the Derridean provocation. Let us therefore follow the argument and the fable of the beginning of *Spurs* quite closely—though only as an introduction to our own postponements.

The book shows thirteen sections. The movement of its thought may be telescoped into three stages: first, an introduction to the questions of truth, writing, style, and woman (roughly, sections 1–6); second, an attempt to pierce the horizon of Heidegger's reading of Nietzsche and Heidegger's own thinking of proximation and propriation (roughly, sections 7–12); and third, a conclusion and two postscripts which reassert the recalcitrance of Nietzsche's styles vis-à-vis any given hermeneutic code.

Yet the book involves the movement of an *image* or *fable* as well, initially in the form of the classic Quintilian metonymy, to wit, "sails" (*voiles*) for sailing ships.[3] The same French word also means "veils," hence covering and concealing. Thus, so far: the sails and veils of sailing ships, whose spars or spurs project from the deck and prow. The sailing ship is the ambiguously female-male image Nietzsche so often invokes in order to suggest both the mystery of woman and the mastery of an emphatically masculine "free spirit." Recall the brave ships of *Daybreak* and *The Gay Science* (3, 331; 480), or the staunch Genoese vessel of "Toward New Seas" (3, 649). The equivocal imagery looms also in passages from *Thus Spoke Zarathustra* (4, 134; 235):

> Have you never seen a sail gliding over the sea, bellied and swollen, trembling with the wind's impetuosity?
> Like a sail, trembling with the spirit's impetuosity, my wisdom glides over the sea—my wild wisdom!
>
> My dream: a bold frigate, half ship, half "Mariah" [*Windsbraut*, a gale; literally, "bride of the wind"], silent as a butterfly, impatient as a falcon. . . .

Spar and sail contract abruptly in Derrida's second and thirteenth sections, assuming the shape(s) of an umbrella. Opened, the umbrella fends off weather; closed, it fends off anyone who gets in the way. Derrida identifies it as the umbrella that Nietzsche "lost" in 1881, an umbrella no hermeneutics can recover.[4] The closed umbrella is reminiscent of a *stylet* or *stylo*, and expresses the relationship of style to writing: the pointed object incises or inscribes a matrix, leaving in its wake a trace—the German *Spur*—that constitutes a line of text.

Finally, the negative of veiling, "unveiling" or "revealing," suggests Heidegger's notion of truth as uncovering and disclosing: *Entdecken, Entbergen, Unverborgenheit*. Derrida allows the figures of sail and veil, spar, spur, and stiletto, parasol and paragua open and shut, to tease an entire range of questions from his readers. Some of these questions will, in a moment, bring us to our own postponements—woman, sensuality, and death.

Derrida selects woman, *la femme*, as his subject for a symposium on Nietzsche's styles. Yet he does so in order to show that these do not amount to the same. They are different, they are other, indeed in such a way that alterity invades both terms: there is, as Nietzsche insists (6, 304–05), a multiplicity of styles but no style *an sich*; and, while there are women, there is no *la femme*, no definite article. Derrida spurs his writing to defend against pure presence, univocal content, "the thing itself, the meaning, the truth," insofar as these things are conjured without differentiation (30/38) and manipulated as "essentializing fetishes" (43/54).[5]

The principal Nietzschean text of *Spurs* is aphorism 60 of *The Gay Science*, "Women and Their Action at a Distance." Derrida inserts into this passage a number of lines from the preceding aphorism (FW, 59, "We Artificers!"). Let us first read the principal aphorism (3, 424–25) without

Derrida's interventions and commentary, interrupting solely in order to introduce one or other of Nietzsche's own terms:

> Women [Die Frauen] and Their Action at a Distance. —Do I still have ears? Am I now but an ear, nothing else besides? Here I stand in the midst of the surging surf [inmitten des Brandes der Brandung], its white flames licking their way to my foot:—from every side it threatens, howls, cries, and screams to me, while in the deepest depths the old earthshaker sings his aria, the muffled sounds of a bellowing bull: he beats out such an earthshaker's measure that the very hearts of these monstrous, weathered rocks tremble in their bodies. Then, suddenly, as though born of nothing, there appears beyond the doorway of this hellish labyrinth, only a few leagues removed,—a great sailing ship, gliding along silent as a ghost. Oh, what ghostly beauty! With what enchantment it grips me! Could it be? Has all the tranquillity and silence in the world embarked on this ship [sich hier eingeschifft]? Does my happiness itself have its seat there in that quiet place, my happier "I," my second, dearly departed [vereweigtes] self? To be, not dead, yet no longer alive? As a ghostlike, silent, gazing, gliding, hovering daimon [Mittelwesen]? To be like the ship which with its white sails skims like a huge butterfly over the dark sea! Yes! To skim over existence! That's it! That would be it!——It seems the noise here has made me a visionary? All great noise causes us to posit our happiness in tranquillity and remoteness [Ferne]. When a man stands in the midst of his noise, in his surf of ploys and plans [Würfen und Entwürfen], he too will see tranquil, enchanting creatures gliding by him: he yearns for the happiness and seclusion of them—it's the women [es sind die Frauen]. He almost imagines that his better self dwells among the women: at these quiet places even the loudest surf would grow still as death and life itself become the dream about life. And yet! And yet! My noble enthusiast, even on the loveliest sailing ship there is so much hubbub, so much noise, and alas, such petty, miserable noise! The magic, the most powerful impact of women is, to speak the language of the philosophers, an action at a distance, actio in distans: to it pertains, in the first place and above all else—distance!

Derrida first intervenes in order to indicate how often Nietzsche appeals in his writings to "the labyrinth of an ear."[6] To be sure, Nietzsche remains fascinated by the ear, as when he stresses the passivity of students in the university who are compelled to be "all ears" (1, 739). Among the fellow-cripples Zarathustra encounters on the bridge to overman, the preeminent figure is, again, "all ear" (see "On Redemption"; 4, 178). And in Ecce Homo (6, 302), proclaiming himself Antichrist and Antidonkey at once, Nietzsche writes:

> We all know—indeed, some of us know it from experience—what a long-ear is. Splendid. I dare to assert that I have the smallest ears. This interests the females to no small degree—I believe they feel better understood by me? . . . I am the antijackass par excellence, and am thereby a world-historical beastie—I am, in Greek, and not only in Greek, the Antichrist. . . .

Derrida proceeds (33/42) to draw attention to an "alto voice" heard in *The Gay Science* (FW, 70), "Mistresses of the Masters," voices that appear to lend to the female the heroic features usually ascribed to the male; further, to the word-play *inmitten des Brandes der Brandung*, the latter word suggesting the surf as it breaks on a spur of land, or against a foot, which is here another kind of spur (34/42);[7] repeating the words *seine Aria singt*, Derrida reminds us that Ariadne is not far off. Indeed, Nietzsche's "Plaint of Ariadne" rises from the shores of Naxos, where Minos' daughter, she of the Labyrinth, longs for the return of her hero or god: we will hear her plaint in chapter one, below, "Ariadne."

Derrida's longest intervention is interposed between the words "the dream about life" and the double interjection "And yet! And yet!" He refers to the following passage from *The Gay Science* (FW, 59; here, as in *Spurs*, considerably abridged):

> *We Artificers!*—When we love a woman [*Weib*] we may well fly into a rage against nature, thinking of all the repulsive naturalnesses [*Natürlichkeiten*] to which every woman is exposed. . . . Here one stops his ears against all physiology and secretly decrees for himself: "I want to hear nothing about human beings' consisting of anything more than *soul and form!*" The human being "under the skin" is for all lovers a horror and an abomination, a blasphemy against God and against Love. . . . It is enough for us to love, hate, desire, sense anything at all—immediately the spirit and force of dream comes over us and we climb the most hazardous winding ways, open-eyed, coolly confronting every danger, up to the rooftops and turrets of fantasy, without a hint of vertigo, as though we were born to clamber—we somnambulists of the day! We artificers! We concealers of naturalness! Moonsick, Godsick! Relentless wanderers, still as death, along heights we do not perceive as heights but as our level plains, our securities!

Here the very highest type of human being, the artist and artificer, *der Künstler*, is confounded with the fantast and even the decadent, the despiser of the body. In a note from this same period (1 [47] 1882; *10*, 23) Nietzsche writes: "In the background of his feelings for a woman, the male still feels *contempt* for the female sex."

We understand somewhat better now Nietzsche's cry for *distance*. Indeed, the ship aphorism dramatizes distance by importing no fewer than six caesurae into its text, one of them a double hiatus ("That would be it!— — It seems the noise. . ."). The patronizing and somewhat jaded skeptic who begins, "My noble enthusiast," has his cue in a doubly distancing "And yet! And yet!" In fact, the entire passage is a measuring of distances, deepest depths, leagues, and thresholds: the oppressive closeness of male noises, muf-

fled, subterranean rumblings; the sudden apparition of silence at a watery remove; the transports of enchantment and ecstasy, the bifurcation of the "I"
into two selves, one of them dearly departed to eternity; the opening up of a
new space in between, for intermediaries and emissaries, like the herma-
phrodites of the mysteries, *Mittelwesen*; a state or condition somewhere between sinking or swimming, an Ikarian hovering or gliding along the line of
horizon. A gulf opens between the apparition that seems fully present—
"That's it!"—and its subjunctive counterpart—"That would be it!" *Das wäre
es!* The long *ä* takes the wind out of the sails of *Das ist es!* (*Cratylus*, 427a.) *Das
wäre es!* means as much as "Well, that's *that!*" Indeed, at this point the narrator appears to return to himself, presumably to his solitary self, invoking
and objectifying his "me": "It seems the noise has made me a visionary?" In a
moment the gulf will open again, however, this time to fracture the narrative
frame altogether by introducing a new narrator, a third second-self: "My noble enthusiast," that third begins. Finally, Derrida himself (37/46) notes the
distance effected by the ironic reference to "the language of the philosophers," the Scholastic *actio in distans*, the translation of *Ferne* into Latinate
Distanz, and the curious spacing and punctuating of these words themselves
by colon, hiatus, spaced type, and exclamation point:

> . . . um die Sprache der Philosophen zu reden, eine Wirkung in die Ferne, eine
> actio in distans: dazu gehört aber, zuerst und vor Allem—D i s t a n z !

Nietzsche's reference to *actio in distans* assumes greater significance
when we note the appearance of that term elsewhere in his works. A number
of remarkable notes from the spring of 1873 (7, 572–79) attribute action at a
distance to *time*. First invoked as a Pythagorean response to Democritean atomism, *actio in distans* becomes the center of an extended reflection in
Nietzsche's notebooks on motion, space, and time. The interaction among
various moments of time can be "explained" only in terms of "*actio in distans*,
that is, by leaping [*durch Springen*]." Nietzsche even inserts a diagram of such
leaps, as though in anticipatory caricature of the Husserlian time-line (7,
579); yet his "dynamic atomism" of time twists on the horns of the ancient
dilemma, stigmatic point *versus* continuous line, without being able to re-
solve it. "But time is not a continuum at all; there are only *totally discrete time-
points, and no line:* Actio in distans."

In "On the Advantage and Disadvantage of History for Life" (UB II, 7;
1, 298) Nietzsche complains that Protestant Christianity has been fatal "to
every spirited *actio in distans*" that occurs in great art and religion, and has
been destructive of "the protecting, veiling vapor" that surrounds and nur-

tures genius. In another note from *The Gay Science* (FW, 15, "Out of the Distance"; *3*, 388) he remarks that the dominant feature of any landscape, for example, a towering mountain, must be viewed from afar; whenever we ascend the mountain, taking it as our vantage-point, we find that the landscape has lost its sublimity and charm. More crucial to our own concerns is a note of 1885 (34[247]; *11*, 504) that identifies *actio in distans* as the operative mode of will to power in nature:

> . . . It is will to power that guides the anorganic world as well; or, rather, . . . there is no anorganic world. "Action at a distance" ["*Die Wirkung in die Ferne*"] cannot be cast aside: *something attracts something else, something feels itself being drawn.* This is the fundamental fact: as opposed to the mechanistic notion of pressure and impact. . . .

Most crucial to this issue of distance is the relation—undiscussed by Nietzsche, as far as I am aware—of *actio in distans* to the central genealogical notion of *Pathos der Distanz*. The latter Nietzsche defines as the essence of nobility, particularly the manly nobility of heroic Hellenes: ἐσθλός is their word for it (5, 263). In the hierarchy of values to be promulgated by the revaluation, the value of *Distanz* is always and everywhere supreme (see 6, 200, 218, 243, 294, 299, and 362). One would have to review quite carefully the entire range of remarks on "distance" in *Beyond Good and Evil* and *Toward a Genealogy of Morals*; for "distance" is what preserves nobility from infectious ressentiment, interiorized cruelty, and decadence.[8] One would also have to contemplate the unsettling fact that *Distanz*, the aura of the feminine, here invades the very essence of heroic masculinity. While Nietzsche's genealogical critique tends to identify the female with the interiorized cruelty and rancor of morality (Nietzsche calls the latter *Circe*), such genealogy can find no purchase on the positive theme of nobility except through *Distanz*. In short, and to summarize everything we have been saying here, nothing Nietzsche says about time, nature, art, will to power, or the nobility that characterizes the "free spirit" can escape from the ambiguity of the aura of distance. The ambiguity of distance is the proximity of ambiguity in the rigging of doublings, folds, and duplicities. "It's the women."

Derrida also emphasizes the word *totenstill* in these passages from *The Gay Science*, "deathly still" suggesting both the *dream* of death and the somnambulant *risk* of death. His reading moves inevitably toward Freud's evocation of *thanatos* in *Beyond the Pleasure Principle* and the extended Lacanian exegesis of that text. The theme of death-castration (by no means foreign to Nietzsche) becomes central for Derrida. Both the dream and risk of death are engaged to the ascensional movement that psychoanalysis calls *genito-*

fugaldisplacement. Ascent is possible only when the member to which the sensuality of woman speaks is extirpated, excised, or excreted; a deadly nostalgia draws the male upward to eternity, to his dearly departed self, beyond the recesses and rhythms of the flesh. It is this seductive, terrifying butterfly and bird of prey which acts at a distance that Derrida conjures in *Spurs.*

The question of feminine distance, of the dream and risk of death, encompasses the entire problem of space and time, the problem of *proximation* as posed in the history of metaphysics, from the "crater" or mixing bowl of Plato's *Timaeus* (the "matrix" and "nurse" of all genesis and the source of all madness and disease) to the phenomenology and poetics of Heidegger (the "undistancing" of finite Dasein and the "withdrawal" of Being as propriation).[9] Derrida traces the question of space (better, *spacing*) and proximation back to the question of truth as unveiling and disclosure; yet the unveiling is itself inaccessible, cannot serve as an ultimate origin or source. Again adopting Heidegger's own words, Derrida invokes the "nontruth of truth";[10] departing from Heidegger's words and ways, he calls the nontruth of truth not *errancy* but *woman.* Yet the aberrant word *woman* distances itself immediately: "There is no essence of woman, because woman diverts herself and is diverted from herself" (38/48). The distancing, diverting, self-veiling, alluring yet terrifying approach and withdrawal of woman becomes Nietzsche's most compelling image of life, *vita femina* (FW, 339; 3, 569). "Yet perhaps this is the most powerful enchantment of life: a gold-embroidered veil of beautiful possibilities lies over it, promising, reticent, demure, taunting, compassionate, seductive. Yes, life is a woman!" "Presupposing that truth is a woman," begins the famous Preface to *Beyond Good and Evil* (5, 11), only to have a later passage (5, 171) drive the wedge between truth and life by retorting, "But she doesn't *want* truth: what does a woman care about truth!" Her talent, "her great art," is the lie; "her supreme affair is semblance and radiance, *der Schein und die Schönheit.*" "Baubo," exclaims the Foreword to the second edition of *The Gay Science,* fecund goddess of the profoundly superficial Greeks: truth is a woman who has good reasons for covering her reasons. And so on.

Yet how daunting all this must be for those women who are not *la femme* but women; who are, that is to say, the only women we know. It is the male philosopher who believes in "woman" and "truth" alike, the male philosopher who, according to both Nietzsche and Derrida, proves credulous, dogmatic, and mistaken. Writing now with the other hand, as it were, both Nietzsche and Derrida record the plaint of women against "the foolishness of the dogmatic philosopher, the impotent artist, or the inexperienced seducer" (43/54):

> Because if woman *is* truth, *she* knows that the truth is not, that the truth does not take place, and that one does not possess the truth. She is woman insofar as she herself does not believe in the truth, does not believe in what she is, in what one believes she is, which, therefore, she is not (40/52).

Thus divested of her identity, an identity that has been imposed on her from the outside, woman can no longer be taken as *the* truth. In itself. Such divestiture leads Derrida once again, constrained as it were by the truth itself, to the theme of castration in Lacanian psychoanalysis.[11] We shall have to skirt this theme, to which we have now been led for the second time, and from which there would be no escape; so that we would never arrive at our own postponements; skirt it by indicating merely that Derrida employs the same strategy here as in the questions of *la femme* and *la vérité*. Woman suspends the truth of castration, which is "men's affair," when she realizes "that castration *does not take place*" (48/60). Except in the project of Christian culture as diagnosed by Nietzsche. Except, that is to say, in the world as we know it.

However, it is not my purpose now to follow on the heels of Derrida's *Spurs*, to take up the role of the feminine in Nietzsche's conception of art or Heidegger's circumvention of woman in this respect. Nor shall I turn elsewhere in Derrida's work to see how the problem of castration and aggressivity leads to the question of bisexuality as such.[12] Nor finally will I examine the ways in which the curious sisterhood of truth, style, and woman affects the Heideggerian notions of the truth of Being, *Ereignis*, and the granting of Time and Being; or the ways in which that sisterhood may well exhaust the possibilities of hermeneutics in general. Except to cite one last tantalizing statement from *Spurs* (86/106):

> From the moment the question of woman suspends the decidable opposition of true and nontrue; inaugurates the epochal regime of scare quotes for all the concepts that pertain to the system of such philosophical decidability; disqualifies the hermeneutical project's postulation of the true meaning of a text; liberates our reading from the horizon of the meaning of Being or the truth of Being, from the values of the production of the product or the presence of the present; from that moment on, what is unchained is the question of style as a question of writing, the question of a spurring operation more powerful than all content, every thesis, and all meaning.

Not to postpone writing this Introduction any longer. To write it now, spurred on, if only by scare quotes. Two questions: What form does the constellation of woman, sensuality, and tragic death take in Nietzsche? And why does Nietzsche postpone confrontation with this complex throughout the two decades of his life as writer and thinker?

Postponements proceeds in four stages, has four chapters. In chapter two, "Corinna," I ask the above questions of Nietzsche's *Birth of Tragedy* and the related unpublished writings of 1870–72. Here my principal texts will be plans for a drama entitled *Empedocles*, plans sketched under the shadow of Hölderlin's three mighty drafts of *The Death of Empedocles*, the drama that so moved Nietzsche when he first read it at age sixteen. In Nietzsche's projected play, though not in Hölderlin's, the leading female character embodies sensual love, plague, and death for the tragic philosopher.

Many elements of Nietzsche's abortive *Empedocles* drama emerge a dozen years later in plans surrounding *Thus Spoke Zarathustra*. Again we find plans for a drama, which now has Zarathustra as its tragic hero. Chapter three, "Pana," focuses on this second set of drama plans. Here once again Nietzsche's heroine combines sensuality, pestilence, and death; but now her presence and her function are essential to the communication of Nietzsche's "thought of thoughts," the eternal recurrence of the same. Nietzsche fails to integrate this female personage into any of the four parts of *Thus Spoke Zarathustra*. To integrate her would be to precipitate Zarathustra's death, to fulfill once and for all his tragic fate. Zarathustra's woman and Zarathustra's death are thus postponed from book to book. Yet they do not disappear entirely from the notebooks—as chapter four, "Calina," will show—until late 1886, and perhaps not until 1888, on the very verge of Nietzsche's collapse.

The names *Corinna*, *Pana*, and *Calina* are not yet familiar to us. The name *Ariadne* we have long known.

In 1935 the German classicist Karl Reinhardt published an article entitled "Nietzsche's 'Plaint of Ariadne.' " His remarkable essay anticipated many of the themes in Derrida's *Spurs*, demonstrating in advance, as it were, that Derrida's is not some far-fetched provocation but a subtle, supple interpretation of an issue that is central to Nietzsche's philosophy. It is striking that Heidegger, in his 1937 lecture course on "The Eternal Recurrence of the Same," encouraged his students to study Reinhardt's piece; highly striking, because no other interpretation so powerfully challenges the Heideggerian reading. There would even be grounds for saying (and in chapter three I shall say it) that Heidegger's entire lecture course is a prolonged response to Reinhardt's thesis. Derrida, himself a painstaking reader of Heidegger's *Nietzsche*, never refers to "Nietzsche's 'Plaint of Ariadne.' " Thus I begin these postponements with an account of "Ariadne."

Chapter one will take us to the end of Nietzsche's career, inasmuch as Ariadne gains ascendancy during the years 1886–89. Chapter two will then leap back to the period of *The Birth of Tragedy*. Chapters three and four will work their way forward once again, from *Thus Spoke Zarathustra* to the eve of Nietzsche's collapse.

Omega's Eyes, 1908–09. Lithograph. Courtesy of The Art Institute of Chicago. Kate S. Buckingham Collection.

CHAPTER ONE

Ariadne

I thought . . . about the labyrinth, and I expected frightful things. . . .

On the table . . . a brightly colored book lay open. I approached and saw . . . burnt sienna. . . . I heard something like the hiss of a thousand serpents, but not frightening, almost seductive, and a woman appeared, bathed in light, and put her face to mine, breathing on me.

—Umberto Eco, *The Name of the Rose*

To the Lady of the Labyrinth, a jar of honey.

—From the Cretan Linear B Scripts

Labyrinth.

A labyrinthine human being never seeks the truth, but—whatever he may try to tell us—always and only his Ariadne.

—4 [55] 1882–83; *10*, 125

In the web of the text Nietzsche is a bit forlorn, like a spider [*araignée*] unequal to what has been produced through her; I say again, like a spider, or several spiders. . . .

He was, he feared, such a castrated woman.
He was, he feared, such a castrating woman.
He was, he loved, such an affirming woman.

—Jacques Derrida, *Spurs*

ACCORDING TO KARL REINHARDT, Nietzsche's *Dionysos Dithyrambs* are songs of inner destiny: they express the tragic conflict of opposing forces in Nietzsche.[1] These "voices" come to speak in Nietzsche's poetry after the mid-1880s "pluralistically, dialogically"; they are multivalent, equivocal, and contradictory (312). Yet the only one of the *Dionysos Dithyrambs* (sketched for the most part in the autumn of 1884, collected and published during the last days of Nietzsche's wakeful life[2]) that is truly Dionysian in content is "The Plaint of Ariadne," *Klage der Ariadne*. And even here the Dionysian symbolism is imposed on an older poem only in the last days of 1888 or the first days of 1889. The first public appearance of the poem is as the song of "The Magician" (or "Sorcerer" or "Wizard": *der Zauberer*) in the fourth and final part of *Thus Spoke Zarathustra* (4, 313–17).

As Reinhardt begins to compare the two published texts (313) the preposterous facts of the case emerge: Nietzsche has changed the sex of the singer, altered the gender of the narrative or incantatory voice of the poem. This change, along with a number of alterations in the prosody (the length of the lines and rhetorical periods is dramatically reduced), totally transforms the impact of the poem. (An important further alteration is the addition of a *coda* in which the god Dionysos himself appears on the scene.) The magician is—and *sounds* like—a yammering ham actor, a half-Christian, half-Romantic God-seeker, who implores his "unknown God." Moreover, his histrionics are—and *sound* as though they are—faked and contrived: the wizard turns out to be one of those poets who lie too much. When the magician's whining is finally over, Zarathustra employs the techniques of our best literary critics: he pummels him with a stick.[3]

Reinhardt's question is how Nietzsche in 1888 could have placed the wizard's undignified hue and cry in the mouth of Ariadne, to whom no one would ever dare take a stick, and he surmises that this bewildering event—unparalleled, he insists, in the history of literature—betrays something of enormous importance. "The change of name would seem enigmatic, bizarre, nonsensical, if it were not possible to trace it back to a more general process, a metamorphosis, a destiny in Nietzsche's entire philosophy of the later period, the period after *Zarathustra*" (315).

Before proceeding, we might try to hear the difference in impact between these two all but identical poems. We will forgo a close comparison of "The Magician's Song" and the "Plaint of Ariadne," which vary only slightly in their appearance on the page. We shall try something else instead: we shall try to put the following words in the mouths, first, of a doddering male histrion, and second, of a beautiful, abandoned woman:

Plaint of Ariadne

Who will warm me, who loves me still?
　Give warm hands!
　give the heart's brazier!
Spread-eagled, shuddering
Like one half dead, whose feet are rubbed;
Racked, oh, by unknown fevers,
trembling at pointed arrows of icy frost,
　shot by you, O thought!
Unnameable! Veiled! Horrific!
　You hunter behind clouds!
Struck down by your lightning,
　scornful eye, gazing on me out of the dark!
　Thus I lie,
turn, twist, tortured
by all the eternal martyrdoms,
　struck

by you, cruellest hunter,
you unknown—god . . .

Strike deeper!
Strike one more time!
Sting, break this heart!
Why this slow martyrdom
of blunt-toothed arrows?
How can you look on,
unweary of human pain,
with the vicious lightning eyes of gods?
You do not wish to kill,
you only would torment, torment?
Why torment—*me*,
you vicious unknown god?

Aha!
You creep up now
at midnight? . . .
What do you want?
Speak!
You crowd close, oppress me,
Ha! already much too close!
You listen to my breathing,
hearken to my heart,
you jealous one!
      —whatever are you jealous of?
Away! Away!
what's the ladder for?
you want to *come in*,
into my heart, you want to enter,
enter my most secret thoughts?
You have no shame!
Unknown! Thief!
What would you steal?
Why would you eavesdrop?
why would you torture,
you torturer!
you—executioner god!
Or shall I, like a dog,
grovel before you?
Devotedly, ecstatically beside myself,
wag my tail—for love of you?
Never fear!
Prick on!

Cruellest thorn!
No dog—I'm but your game,
cruellest hunter!
your proudest prisoner,
you highwayman behind clouds . . .
Why don't you say something!
Veiled in lightning! Unknown! speak!
Waiting in ambush: what do you want
of—*me*? . . .

What's that?
Ransom?
Why a ransom?
Ask for a lot—my pride adjures you!
and say little—my second pride adjures you

Aha!
Me?—you want me?
　—all of me? . . .

Aha!
And you torment me, fool that you are,
you mortify my pride?
Give me *love*—who warms me still?
　who loves me still?
give warm hands,
give the heart's brazier,
give me, the loneliest one,
whom ice, oh, ice sevenfold
teaches to languish for enemies,
languish for enemies,
give, yes, give me,
cruellest enemy,
your—*self*! . . .

Gone!
He has fled,
my sole companion,
my magnificent enemy,
my unknown,
my executioner god! . . .
No!
come back!
With all your martyrdoms!
All my tears run their course
and flow to you,
and the last flames of my hear'

flicker for you.
Oh, come back,
my unknown god! my *agony!*
   my ultimate happiness! . . .

A lightning bolt. Dionysos becomes visible
in emerald beauty.

     Dionysos:

Be clever, Ariadne! . . .
You have little ears; you have my ears:
stick a clever word in them!—
Must one not first hate oneself
   in order to love oneself? . . .
I am your labyrinth. . . .

A wizard blasted by lightning is a mere parody of Hölderlin's destiny; a woman so struck is Hölderlin's august and tragic Semele. A toothless sorcerer writhing on the ground is sheer burlesque; a breathtaking heroine, twisting, tortured, is no laughing matter.

Yet one magnificent woman is not another, and it is time to complicate the picture still further. Although Reinhardt is unaware of it, the fact is that the transformation of wizard to woman is the *second* change the poem underwent. In its original form the plaint was sung by a woman, a woman in childbirth; so that the change from magician to maid is actually a *restoration* of sorts. Not surprisingly, the poetic fragments in question (see especially 28 [9, 12, and 27] 1884; *11*, 301–03; 310) manifest a split in point-of-view. "Who are *you* waiting for . . . *you* despairing one . . . ah, how *you* lament!" says one fragment (my emphases). But then: "Oh, warm me! love me . . . ."

I lie still—
spread-eagled,
like one half dead, whose feet
   must be rubbed
—the pretty little things are afraid
of me . . . .[†]

In the twelfth fragment we read the phrase *Qual des Schaffens*, "the travail of creation." We then arrive at a poem given the number 6 and entitled, "The Poet—The Creator's Travail." The poet (the proper identity of the charlatan wizard) and the creator suffer in the way indicated by the poem's original title (*14*, 711), *Die Qual der Gebärerin*, "The Travail of the Woman in Childbirth." The number 6 designates the poem's place in a projected collection of "Hymns to Medusa." Medusa, who will rear her head on several occasions during these postponements, making matters congeal.

The title *Qual der Gebärerin* emerges four years later in *Twilight of the Idols* (1888; 6, 159). The context there is the tradition of orgiastic ritual in ancient Greece. (It is a tradition we will confront in chapter two, "Corinna," during our discussion of *The Birth of Tragedy*, even though Nietzsche himself postponed discussion of it until the late 1880s.) Such rituals reenact "the eternal recurrence of life" and thus form the core of the Dionysian and Eleusinian mysteries. The enigmas of sexuality harbor the symbols of Greek piety as such, whether these be the phallus or any other "particulars" of procreation, pregnancy, and birth:

> In the mystery doctrines *pain* was proclaimed holy: the "contractions [*Wehen*] of the woman in childbirth" sanctify pain in general: all becoming and growing, all nurture of the future *conditions* pain. . . . In order for the eternal joy of creation to be granted, in order for the will to life to affirm itself eternally, the "travail [*Qual*] of the woman in childbirth" must also be granted. . . . All this is signified in the word *Dionysos*: I know no higher symbolism than this Greek symbolism, the symbolism of the Dionysian.

Karl Reinhardt now pursues (316–18) the multiple figures and voices of the sundry *Dionysos Dithyrambs*, especially the voices of overcoming and submission. In and after *Thus Spoke Zarathustra* these voices achieve supreme consonance, whatever conflicts there may be. For both the genealogist and the "Dionysian philosopher" alike, overcoming is always a self-overcoming; the domain of the hunt is always the home of the hunter himself; the measure of the prize is always in pounds of the hunter's own flesh. Reinhardt thus resists the temptation to trace the conflicts of Nietzsche's "inner drama" or the "riddle of the duplicity in him" back to some doctrine of "split personality" or to Nietzsche's "Protestant legacy" (320–21). He tries to understand instead how Nietzsche is able actually to speak with the voice of woman, the voice in the throat of woman. And he tries to understand why this should be necessary.

For Reinhardt, the crucial text is Nietzsche's "Philosophy of the Future," that is to say, *Beyond Good and Evil*, and particularly its concluding sections. Here Dionysos is no longer the passive victim of joy and suffering but the active "tempter-god." Here, according to Reinhardt, a new world is in the making. Not the world of *Welt-Spiel* but the "primal tragedy-plus-comedy" of the god Dionysos. Not that the innocence and joy of Becoming are abandoned for the sake of Being: Nietzsche's "hymn of invocation" to

Dionysos (JGB, 295) radiates golden laughter. Dionysos is "a tempter-god and born Pied Piper of the conscience," a god of "allurement" whose generosity causes his followers to become "richer in themselves, newer than before, freshly opened, warmed by a thawing wind that harkens to every word," more fragile than ever before "yet full of hopes that as yet have no name, full of new will and flow, turnings-away and eddyings" (5, 237). Precisely in the years 1885–86, after the sunburst of *Zarathustra*, Nietzsche envisages a return to his own Dionysian origins. To a list of his published works drawn up early in 1885 (*11*, 351) he adds the title, "*Dionysos, or: The Sacred Orgies.*" At the same time he begins to ruminate on his first-born, *The Birth of Tragedy*, a book possessed of "an intellectuality that works on the senses" (*11*, 357). These ruminations will of course culminate in the famous "Attempt at a Self-Criticism" of 1886. "In the meantime," notes Nietzsche, referring to the years 1872 to 1885, the crucial period for these postponements, "I have learned a great deal, really too much, about this god's philosophy; and, as I said, from mouth to mouth [N. B.: not from mouth to ear]—I, the last disciple and initiate of the god Dionysos" (5, 238). Reinhardt makes much of this new role for the god, *Dionysos philosophos*, a role Nietzsche himself celebrates as something "secret, new, alien, marvelous, uncanny" (5, 238):

> The very fact that Dionysos is a philosopher, and thus that gods too philosophize, seems to me a not altogether harmless novelty, one that may induce mistrust precisely among philosophers —among you, my friends, it will surely be found less objectionable, unless it should come too late, or at an unpropitious hour: for I have been told that these days you are reluctant to believe in God and gods.

Holding forth in the same style, Nietzsche informs us that he has had conversations with the god, troublesome conversations, inasmuch as Dionysos flaunts his glory in unaccustomed ways, feeling no need to clothe his nakedness.

> One must surmise: Does this kind of godhead and philosopher perhaps lack shame?—He once said to me, "If the circumstances are right, I love human beings." He was alluding here to Ariadne, who happened to be present. "Human beings are pleasant, brave, inventive animals, as far as I am concerned; they have no equals on earth, and can find their way about in all labyrinths. I am good to them: I often think about how I can bring them farther along and make them stronger, more wicked and more profound than they are."— "Stronger, more wicked and profound?" I asked, horrified. "Yes," he repeated, "stronger, more wicked and more profound; also more beautiful." So saying, the tempter-god smiled his halcyon smile, as if he had uttered some delightful civility. One discerns immediately that it is not only shame that this divinity

lacks—; and in general we have good grounds for asseverating that in some respects the gods as a whole might profitably go to school amongst us humans. We human beings are—more human. . . (5, 238–39; cf. *11*, 481–83).

Whether we will want to read these ironic and disingenuous accounts of Nietzsche's chats with the insolent, lascivious godhead in the way Reinhardt does (321–23), namely, as Nietzsche's farewell to Zarathustra-the-godless and embrace of a new theology and mystery religion, is surely questionable, whatever Reinhardt's own assurances. "There is no doubt about it," Reinhardt insists: "Dionysos-as-philosopher is a preliminary taste of a new myth, one that replaces, cancels, and surpasses Zarathustra's 'overman' " (323). Reinhardt's principal grounds for his thesis concerning the radical change in Nietzsche's thinking after *Thus Spoke Zarathustra*, grounds we shall have to test in chapter three, "Pana," are the plans surrounding that very book. According to Reinhardt, these plans betray the fact that whereas Zarathustra was originally conceived of as one who *goes down* tragically and ineluctably, he eventually becomes one "who contentedly goes over," and perhaps even upward, into an open future. Zarathustra is ultimately no *Untergehender*, says Reinhardt, but a *Hinübergehender*.[4] After 1885 Nietzsche therefore requires another, more tragic avatar. Hence the "Plaint of Ariadne."

Alas, the epiphany of Dionysos in that poem turns out to be boundlessly disappointing. For after establishing the pathos of Ariadne's torment the poem ushers in a dandyish Dionysos who contents himself with a few sententious remarks. Even though Ariadne has the god's ear, Dionysos dispenses his unsolicited advice and appropriates her Labyrinth. What he lacks is not shame but style.

Reinhardt rightly invokes the "Ass Festival" of *Thus Spoke Zarathustra*, Part IV, and the *adventavit asinus* of *Beyond Good and Evil* (aphorism 8). He might also have mentioned Nietzsche's own pirating of the lines "Ask for a lot . . . /and say little" for one of his cheeky "Seven Little Maxims on Woman" (JGB 237; 5, 174): "It says a lot, yet is quite still—that's thin ice for an ass named Jill." Yet no such "scholarly" references rescue the "Plaint." Quite the reverse. When Dionysos arrogates the Labyrinth to himself, leaving Ariadne with a clever word stuck in her ear, all is *displaced* in a satyr-play which for all its forced jollity is woefully out of place, meager, and embarrassing. Whatever Nietzsche's *vision* of Dionysos and Ariadne may be, concedes Reinhardt (331), all *communication* of it fails: *Die Sprache versagt sich*, the language refuses to speak, botches its own telling, squanders its powers. By 1888 Nietzsche has stopped writing poetry and begun to legislate, hammer, and annihilate. Reinhardt comments on Nietzsche's use of language in the late 1880s as follows:

> The multiple layers, the enchantments, terrors, sorrows, and felicities of a nurtured pluralism disappear behind an increasingly *ad hoc* will to engage, to exert power; the language itself, except when reminiscences irradiate it, becomes monotonous, univocal, loses its shimmer and the oscillations of its hues; it becomes brittle under the regime of glaring lights, grows drastic, "cynical," plaintive, peremptory, declamatory.

Nevertheless, it is not the *failure* that Reinhardt wishes to stress. For Nietzsche's *effort* remains astonishing, the effort Reinhardt throughout his article calls *die Umtaufe*, "the rechristening" of the magician—which of course is his dechristening and radical transmutation into Ariadne. If Dionysos disappoints, Ariadne enthralls. For what engages our attention is not simply the fact that "a feminine is inserted in place of a masculine" (326) but the possibility that a metamorphosis is occurring in Nietzsche's thinking as a whole. That the butterfly withers in the chrysalis no one would deny. Yet precisely why that development is thwarted, why the transition to Ariadne in agony is postponed again and again, is the question we must sustain. If we now allow the most famous passages on Dionysos and Ariadne in Nietzsche's works to pass in review, and then turn to the less familiar jottings in the notebooks, we may be able to deepen that question as well.

Immensely important for this question are Nietzsche's remarks—to which I can do no justice here—on the psychology and physiology of Dionysian rapture, *Rausch*.[5] Nietzsche contrasts Apollinian "rapture of the eye" with Dionysian ecstasy; the latter is total rapture, "metamorphosis" whole and entire. Mimicry, dramatic involvement, histrionics, and something at least resembling hysterics are its earmarks. To the observations made earlier on the "travail of the woman in childbirth" Nietzsche adds that the psychology of orgiastic experience provides "the key to the concept of *tragic* feeling" (6, 160). Not the catharsis of fear and pity typifies tragedy, but a feeling by which one becomes oneself "the eternal joy of Becoming" as well as the joy of "annihilation."[6]

> And therewith I touch again on the very place I started from: *The Birth of Tragedy* was my first revaluation of all values. Thus I move back to the ground from which my willing, my *ability*, waxes—I, the last disciple of the philosopher Dionysos—I, the teacher of eternal return. . . (6, 180).

The same cluster of themes emerges in *Ecce Homo*. In the book's Preface Nietzsche introduces himself as "a disciple of the philosopher Dionysos" and states his preference for satyrhood over sainthood (6, 258). In his account of *The Birth of Tragedy* he proclaims himself "the first *tragic philosopher*," one whose tragic wisdom (the wisdom of Heraclitus or, we might add, of Empedocles) enables him "to transpose the Dionysian into a philosophical pathos" (6, 312). Perhaps such pathos resembles the pathos of *distance*, inasmuch as the Dionysian unites joy in birth and in annihilation, thus going the distance between these opposites.

Yet it is in his retrospect on *Thus Spoke Zarathustra* that Nietzsche has a great deal to say about Dionysos. The Dionysian "here became supreme deed," because *Zarathustra* was not only *about* Dionysos but, as Nietzsche's analysis of inspiration indicates (6, 339–42), *of* Dionysos. As a conjunction of radical opposites, Zarathustra feels himself to be "the *supreme form of all being.*"

> *But this is the very concept of Dionysos.*—Another consideration as well leads us there. The psychological problem in the Zarathustra-type is how he who to an unprecedented degree says "no," *performs* "no" to everything that up to now people have said "yes" to, can nonetheless be the opposite of a no-saying spirit; how the most burdensome destiny, the fatality of a spirit saddled with a task, can nonetheless be the lightest and most transcendent of characters—Zarathustra is a dancer; how the one who has the hardest, most frightful insight into reality, has thought the "most abysmal thought," nonetheless finds there no objection to existence, not even to its eternal return; who rather finds it yet another reason *himself to be* the eternal yes to all things, "the vast, boundless utterance of yes-and-amen." "Into all abysses I bear my blessing yes-saying still". . . . *But once again that is the concept of Dionysos* (6, 344–45).

It is difficult to demur from Reinhardt's judgment—indeed a kind of consensus rules here in Nietzsche interpretation, where consensus is exceedingly rare—that Nietzsche's performance of the "no" began to consume more and more of him after *Zarathustra*, began to smother the "yes." Later in *Ecce Homo* (6, 366) we find Nietzsche portraying his "Dionysian nature" strictly in terms of "the joy in *annihilation*," in a style whose bravado is reminiscent of no one so much as Pentheus. Pentheus quitting Thebes, under way to his own peculiar rechristening. The bravado goes hand-in-hand with facetiousness concerning woman, woman-in-itself, "eternal" woman.

> By the by, may I put forward the proposition that I *know* females? It pertains to my Dionysian dowry. Who knows, I may be the first psychologist of the eternal feminine? They all love me—it's an old story—with the exception of the *botched* females, the "emancipated" ones, who no longer have what it takes to bear children [*das Zeug zu Kindern*]. —Luckily, I am not willing to let myself be torn to pieces: the complete woman tears to pieces when she loves. . . . I know

these lovable Maenads. . . . Ah, what dangerous, slithering, subterranean little carnivores! And so pleasant all the while! (6, 305–06).

Passages like this one impale us on the horns of a dilemma, one that Nietzsche himself, lest he be adjudged "medi-cynical," never confronts directly, never elucidates. The incomplete woman, the "botched" (*verunglückte*) female who cannot be made pregnant and thus defused and domesticated, the castrating woman, Nietzsche abhors; yet the "complete" or "perfect" woman, *das vollkommene Weib*, who is eminently eligible and who has what it takes, tears apart and devours. Whether she is publicist or tigress, Maud Gonne behind either of her faces, the outcome is the same. Hence the terrific recoil of the word *Maenad* here: Nietzsche celebrates a Dionysian philosophy that would banish the flute girls and persecute the Maenad worshipers! The facetiousness and forced jollity of the style perhaps betray the fact that Nietzsche perceives the redoubtable double jeopardy of his own situation. In the very passage that disperses the Maenads Nietzsche reveals the goal and essence of the philosophical idealism he opposes as the "poisoning" of the "good conscience and the naturalness in sexual love," the same naturalness that instigated horror in "us artificers." He refers his reader to Article Four of his "Proscription of Christianity" (6, 254; 307):

> To preach chastity is public incitement to unnatural acts. All contempt of sexual life and all besmirching of the same through use of the concept "impurity" is the capital crime against life—the genuine sin against the Holy Spirit of life.

Yet Nietzsche's most candid and lucid statement concerning woman and sensual love—to pretend for a moment that candor and lucidity might ever suffice here—brings him as close to the Christ as he ever came. *Beyond Good and Evil*, number 269 (5, 224–25):

> . . . Woman would like to believe that love can do *everything*; this is her proper *faith*. Alas, knowers of the heart will surmise how poor, dullwitted, helpless, presumptuous, blundering—how much more likely to destroy than to rescue—even the best, most profound love is! It is possible that behind the sacred fable and disguise of the Life of Jesus one of the most painful cases of martyrdom arising from *knowledge about love* lies concealed: the martyrdom of the most innocent and yearning heart, which was never satisfied by any human love, which *demanded* love, to be loved and nothing else; a heart that turned on those who refused to love in return, turned in hardness, madness, and frightful rage; the history of a poor wretch who was never sated, never satisfied in love, who had to invent an Inferno to which he could despatch those who *refused* to love him—and who finally, having learned about human love, had to invent a God who is all love, pure potentiality-for-love, a God who has mercy on human love because it is so flimsy, so incompetent! Whoever feels this way, whoever *knows*

such things about love, *seeks* death. —But why insist on such painful things? Assuming that one need not do so.

Martyrdom is the refrain that echoes in the mouths of both the sorcerer-poet and Ariadne. Here Nietzsche's writing on love—human love, womanly love, sensual love—brings him closer to death, the emblem of the Crucified, than to Dionysian life. Here no bravado, nothing for show. "Such painful things," set off by caesurae, in distantiation and displacement, are the very stuff of postponements.

In the final two sections of the retrospect on *Zarathustra* in *Ecce Homo* we find an equally insightful yet more affirmative Nietzsche. It is not surprising that the leading figure of these passages is neither the Crucified nor Dionysos but Ariadne. During the winter of 1882–83 Nietzsche had jotted the following note (*10*, 125):

> Labyrinth.
> A labyrinthine human being never seeks the truth, but—whatever he may try to tell us—always and only his Ariadne.

And we know that the manuscript of *Thus Spoke Zarathustra*, Part III, had as the title of the episode now called "On the Great Longing" (which begins, "O my soul . . . ") the name *Ariadne*. We also know that preceding the words of the title "The Other Dance Song" appeared the rubric *Vita femina* (*14*, 324). By autumn of 1888, when Nietzsche composes *Ecce Homo*, Ariadne is omnipresent. "In the midst of martyrdoms," *Mitten in Martern*, writes Nietzsche in "Why I Am So Wise" (*6*, 265), applying to the story of his own illness the vocabulary of Ariadne's lament. In the sections immediately following his description of the Zarathustra-type Nietzsche brings forward Zarathustra's "Nightsong" as an exemplum of Dionysian dithyramb. He calls it a plaint or lament, *eine Klage*, indeed of one who is "condemned not to love" (*6*, 345). The lament emanates a "divine tenderness" and incandesces with the very hue of Dionysos-Ariadne: Nietzsche refers to the dithyramb's "emerald felicity." The opening lines of "The Nightsong":

> It is night: now all leaping fountains talk aloud. And my soul too is a leaping fountain.
> It is night: only now do all lovers' songs stir. And my soul too is a lover's song.
> An unsated, insatiable thirst is in me; it wants to be voiced. A craving for love is in me; it speaks the very language of love.
> I am light: O that I were night! But this is my loneliness—that I am girded in light.
> O that I were dark and of the night! How I would suck at breasts of light!

"Nothing like this was ever poetized, felt, or *suffered* before: thus suffers a god, a Dionysos" (6, 348), Nietzsche exclaims. Yet we recall that in "Plaint of Ariadne" Dionysos does not suffer at all; the travail is Ariadne's, and in response to it the god dispenses clever maxims. The cleverest of words, "I am your Labyrinth," is cleverest because it hides what the labyrinthine human being seeks always and everywhere, cleverest because it almost convinces us that the god answers his own question and is without need. "The Nightsong" is not so clever. "The answer to such a dithyramb of solar solitude, of loneliness in light, would be Ariadne. . . . Who apart from me knows what Ariadne is!"

The answer to Dionysian suffering is not at all the smug Dionysos of the *coda* but mortal Ariadne herself. When the retrospect on *Zarathustra* closes with the command "Become hard!" (the very command that comes to dominate the plans for *Thus Spoke Zarathustra*, discussed in chapter three, "Pana," below), we do not know whether Ariadne smiles or frowns. Yet even if she smiles, it will have been the rueful smile of compassion tinged with contempt.

Karl Reinhardt invites us to consider two very different kinds of failure in Nietzsche's Ariadnic project. On the one hand, he asserts that Nietzsche's notion of a Dionysian *philosophy* is reminiscent not so much of Heraclitus and Empedocles as of their "speculative, even Stoic, then Neo-Platonic transformations" (325). On the other hand, "the enigma of that rechristening" by which the wizard becomes Ariadne peters out in satyr-play. Dionysian philosophy remains intellectualistic, "reflexive," and the Ariadnic mystery is "something displaced" (331). Yet these two are in fact one: displacement seeks sanctuary in reflexive interiority.

Such *displacement* is what these *postponements* are about—except that here there is no sanctuary, but only the Labyrinth. The plans for an Empedoclean drama and Zarathustran play, whether *Trauerspiel* or satyr-play, are themselves displacements. Displacements that keep Nietzsche on track, following the thread. In spite of himself. For the dismemberment of Dionysos Zagreus in some mysterious way leads to the travail of Ariadne.

Reinhardt adjures us not to underestimate the difficulty we will have in following this thread. We might therefore at the end of our reading of his article pause to consider one case of such underestimation—in a writer of unusual perspicacity: Gilles Deleuze, in *Nietzsche et la philosophie*.[7] For Deleuze would want to reply to Reinhardt, would want to insist that Nietzsche's philosophy of Dionysos is a resounding success, that it ably integrates the figure of Ariadne into its project.

For Deleuze, as for Reinhardt, the introduction of Ariadne into the Dionysian philosophy is of crucial importance. Deleuze argues that *The Birth of Tragedy* remains trapped in a "Christian-dialectical" mode of thinking, a thinking in terms of "justification, redemption, and reconciliation" (13). Nietzsche breaks free of such thought, according to Deleuze, when he replaces the dialectical pair Apollo-Dionysos with a twofold opposition, namely, Dionysos *versus* the Crucified, and Dionysos plus Ariadne. Deleuze is able to define the first opposition straightforwardly, since the Crucified is identified with reaction, no-saying, vengeance, and passive nihilism. The second pair, the Ariadnic complement, proves to be more recalcitrant.

In place of the antithesis of Apollo-Dionysos, Deleuze invokes "the more mysterious complementarity of Dionysos-Ariadne" (16). The reason for the substitution is that "a woman, a fiancée, is needed whenever it is a matter of affirming life" (16). Yet who is Ariadne? Deleuze traces her cosmic imagery, the emblems of divinity that Dionysos confers on her: the jewels of her crown are the night stars, constellations formed by her mate's toss of the dice, the single *coup de dés* of chance and necessity (21). It is Dionysos who casts the dice of eternal recurrence; yet the mystery of Ariadne is said to be "Nietzsche's positive secret" (23).

Deleuze cites Nietzsche's pejorative remarks concerning Eve in *The Birth of Tragedy* (we shall hear them in chapter two, "Corinna," below), but he strives to banish Eve's shadow. "There is no Nietzschean misogyny," he insists. "Ariadne is Nietzsche's uppermost secret, the premier feminine power, the Anima, the fiancée who is inseparable from Dionysian affirmation" (24). We will revert to this "premier power" in a moment. But Deleuze goes on to postulate a "second" feminine power, one that embodies the negation of the first (although he refrains from using this dialectical expression): it is the "infernal, negative, and moralizing feminine, the terrifying mother, mother of good and evil, who denigrates and negates life" (24). As though in anticipation of those recently discovered pages of *Ecce Homo* (mentioned in the Introduction, p. 3), Deleuze identifies the "second" feminine power as "our mothers and our sisters." Deleuze's deduction is curious, inasmuch as Eve (wearing the mask of Lilith) is Adam's nefarious mate, not his mother or sister. As his mate, she is more subtly destructive than the Titans, to be sure, and she is certainly difficult to contain.

Deleuze does not play with the name *Ariadne* as Derrida and Nietzsche do.[8] Yet something similar and even more disconcerting happens to Deleuze's text. Precisely at the point where he is discussing the "toss of the dice," trying to preserve the premier feminine power from the depredations of the second, Deleuze employs a signifier that refuses to stay in place. The French *Ariane* is mocked again and again by an *araignée*, the arachnid of reason and morality, the "universal spider" of ressentiment and reaction (see 29, 31, 34–35, and 42). Whereas Deleuze wishes to gaze on the "dancing star" of Ariadne's tiara, the *araignée* of interiorized cruelty weaves its dark web across Deleuze's text.[9]

The significance of this not entirely accidental signification (*Ariane/araignée*) is that "genealogical critique" and "affirmative thought" are not as easy to rescue from their Christian-dialectical matrix as Deleuze hopes. He begins by stressing the fact (or hope) that genealogy's "natural aggressivity" prevails beyond all vengefulness or reaction of any kind (3); he eventually comes to recognize, if only fleetingly, the duplicitous parentage of genealogy itself (40). Nietzsche himself never lost sight of the forked genealogy of genealogy. When Deleuze exalts Nietzschean thought as thinking "that ultimately expels all negativity" (41), and when he identifies tragic thinking as unalloyed joy of affirmation, he suppresses the ambivalence of genealogical critique—suppresses the very quality that makes it nondialectical. In Nietzsche's career of thought, the *negative* opposition (or contraposition) of Dionysos and the Crucified obtains; the *positive* complementarity of Dionysos and Ariadne, the "Dionysian dowry," the agony of dismemberment, is displaced and postponed.

Thus the *who?* question of genealogy is the tragic question *par excellence*. Dionysos, god of metamorphosis, is always the answer, says Deleuze: "In Nietzsche's literary production, the admirable poem 'Plaint of Ariadne' expresses this fundamental rapport between a manner of questioning and the divine personage who is present beneath all the questions—the rapport between the pluralist question and Dionysian or tragic affirmation" (88). Yet if this is so, how is Deleuze or anyone else to preserve the distinction between the first and second feminine powers? What about this "fiancée" and her starry diadem? If Ariadne is sheer affirmation, what has she to complain about? Why the thousand martyrdoms? Very strange things happen to genealogy when the answer to the *who?* question is *Ariane*.

Later in his book Deleuze chastises the magician in the way Zarathustra himself does. The sorcerer is a counterfeit, a mountebank "who fabricates his suffering in order to arouse pity" (189). In a bizarre turnabout, Deleuze scolds the wizard-poet as a betrayer of Dionysos: "He seizes the song of Ariadne; he, the fake tragedian." Whereas of course it is Ariadne who arrogates the wizard's words. Yet Deleuze is more correct than he knows: we have seen that the earliest sketches of the sorcerer's song attribute that plaint to a woman in childbirth. At all events, the matter at stake is a difference between two kinds of suffering, one ostentatious and complacent, the other ecstatic and creative. Ariadne's is the "unknown joy" of the "unknown god"; her travail is wholly affirmative (199). In his eagerness to salvage affirmation from negation and nihilism, Deleuze is blithe about, and even blind to, Ariadne's suffering. He is deaf to her keen.

The Deleuzean rhapsody of *Ariane fiancée* reaches its apotheosis in the last two sections of *Nietzsche et la philosophie* (213–22). Here Ariadne is identified as a full partner in the "double affirmation" of Dionysos-Ariadne, though surely not the senior partner. Dionysos affirms Becoming as Being; Ariadne affirms the god's affirmation. The redoubling of affirmation is essential in Deleuze's view. Yet the necessity of double affirmation remains as obscure as the mystery of mythic Ariadne herself. As the beloved of Theseus, the hero who represents the Higher Man, who takes up challenges and defeats monsters, Ariadne is less than her proper self (214–15):

> Insofar as woman loves man, insofar as she is mother, sister, and spouse of man, even if it be of the Higher Man, she is merely the feminine image of man: feminine power remains captive within woman. [Here Deleuze cites *Thus Spoke Zarathustra*, Part III, "On the Attenuating Virtue."] Terrible mothers, terrible sisters and spouses, femininity here represents the spirit of revenge and the ressentiment that animates man himself. Yet Ariadne abandoned by Theseus senses a nascent transmutation that is proper to her: feminine power set free, become beneficent and affirmative, become Anima.

The "second" feminine power, the monstrous power of the negative, now expands to include the role of spouse, the figure of Eve. The liberation of the woman in woman is to be something utterly new and unheard of: it is to be the very matrix of *Übermensch*. Yet the emancipated power of woman dons the motherliest and sisterliest of ancient masks—virgin Anima, Hagia Sophia, the "soul" with which Zarathustra, shunning his destiny, communes.[10] As though Ariadne's mate were unencumbered *Geist*. Deleuze calls *Ariane-Anima* "a second affirmation," one that takes Dionysian affirmation as its "object." Yet is the "second affirmation" entirely emancipated from the "second power" of woman? Merely to insist on their absolute segregation, simply to assert the affirmative power of Ariadne ("Ariadne is the fiancée, the loving feminine power," 215), is to adopt a position hopelessly outside the Nietzschean problematic. Nietzsche could never have sustained such naïveté.

Deleuze abides by the subordination of Ariadne to Dionysos. The god teaches her *his* secret: "*I am your Labyrinth.*" Deleuze misconstrues the "Plaint of Ariadne" in such a way that it is Ariadne who puts an "appropriate word" in the god's ear: "Having herself heard and understood Dionysian affirmation, she makes it the object of a second affirmation which Dionysos hears" (216). Thus, according to Deleuze, the play of the *difference* in affirmation is "elevated to the highest power" (217). However, with all negativity selected out, and with Ariadne's purely affirmative power defined exclusively as a "mirror, fiancée, or reflection" of Dionysos, what becomes of Ariadne's tortured and tortuous self? What of the Labyrinth, which the fragmented god too seeks and desires? How is Deleuze's "double affirmation" to avoid the traps and trappings of dialectical thinking? When "all negativity is conquered or transmuted" (219), do we find ourselves outside dialectic or on its traditional trajectory toward reconciliation? Ariadne may well be "the unconditional fiancée of Dionysos" (220), yet is it not Nietzsche who inculcates in us suspicion concerning all things "unconditional"? And is not this fiancée a bride-to-be, a spouse, sister, and mother in the making?

The mystery of Ariadne is not so readily unraveled.[11] It will occasion a considerable variety of postponements, here given the names *Corinna, Pana, Calina.* Masks of the Ariadnic enigma. Writing of this mystery in the mid-1930s, Karl Reinhardt, as follows:

> In order to decipher the meaning of the mystery one would have to expound the doctrine of the "great danger," of the "courage to face the forbidden," of the "predestination to the Labyrinth" (Foreword to *The Antichrist*); further, one would have to unravel the entire Ariadnically intricate problem of the mask that looks on itself as a mask, the text that interprets itself as interpretation, the thread that leads us out and then back to our own hand; in short, one would have to unravel the whole problem of Nietzsche's later thinking, the problem of the *circulus vitiosus deus* (330).

Nude Figure (Sin), 1901. Lithograph. Collection, The Museum of Modern Art, New York. Gift of James Thrall Soby.

CHAPTER TWO

Corinna

Concluding Chorus of Act I
Sketch

New world
 and it hangs like a brazen vault
the heaven above us; curse lames
the limbs of all, and the invigorating, glad
gifts of Earth are so much straw; she
taunts us with presents, our Mother
and all is illusion—
O when, when
 already it pours free
 flooding the arid land

Yet where is he?

 That he conjure the living spirit
 —Friedrich Hölderlin, *The Death of Empedocles*, third draft, ca. 1800

And we shall feel the agony of thirst,
The ineffable longing for the life of life
Baffled for ever; and still thought and mind
Will hurry us with them on their homeless march,
Over the unallied unopening earth,
Over the unrecognising sea; while air
Will blow us fiercely back to sea and earth,
And fire repel us from its living waves.
And then we shall unwillingly return
Back to this meadow of calamity,
This uncongenial place, this human life;
And in our individual human state
Go through the sad probation all again,
To see if we will poise our life at last,
To see if we will now at last be true
To our own only true, deep-buried selves,
Being one with which we are one with the whole
 world. . . .
 —Matthew Arnold, *Empedocles on Etna*,
 1852, Act II, ll. 356–72

THE FIRST SENTENCE of the first section of *The Birth of Trag-edy* reads as follows:

> We will have attained much for aesthetic science when we have arrived at not only the logical insight but also an immediate certitude of intuition with regard to the fact that the continuous development of art is bound up with the duplicity of the Apollinian and the Dionysian: in a way that is similar to the way in which generation depends on the duality of the sexes, in perdurant struggle, with only intermittent reconciliation.

"Aesthetic science" is the oxymoron that captures the precarious sense of

Nietzsche's magnificent, mysterious early work as a whole. In this chapter I shall have to skirt the oxymoron, avoiding the troublesome question as to whether and how Nietzsche successfully mates αἰσθητική with ἐπιστήμη, that is, whether and how Nietzsche overcomes the strict segregation of these two in the universe of Plato's *Timaeus* and in the realm of subsequent Western metaphysics. Instead, I shall ask a straightforward, nontechnical question: Precisely how are Apollo and Dionysos to meet and mate, and in such a way as to give birth to tragedy? Who will be the *mother* of tragedy?[1]

Nietzsche invokes the Schopenhauerian "mothers of Being," *Wahn, Wille und Wehe*—will o' the wisp, will, and woe. He also refers to music as the "maternal womb" of tragedy. Yet what do these "mothers" have to do with Apollo and Dionysos? These two gods are stylistic opposites. They comprise the duplicitous source of all Greek art. When they couple, the highest form of Greek art, Attic tragedy, is born. Yet each of these parents, as Nietzsche describes them in *The Birth* and in essays preceding *The Birth*, is itself duplicitous.

Apollo lends his name to the realm of oneiric visibility, pictorial image, outline and measure, limit and individuation. An artist's Apollinian dreamplay produces what Nietzsche calls *den schönen Schein*, radiant semblance. Such play transforms all horror and disgust into beautiful appearance. Yet the transformation is itself duplicitous, inasmuch as a sensation of semblance *as such* accompanies it. Hence a form of knowledge (albeit a knowledge defined by the less-than-Apollinian term sensation, *Empfindung*) must at least accompany, if not help to accomplish, the transmutation of horror. Inasmuch as Nietzsche always and everywhere refers to such horror as insight (*Einblick*) into or knowledge (*Erkenntnis*) of existence, we have the odd situation whereby one kind of knowledge accompanies the semblance that was meant to obscure knowledge, accompanies it without destroying it. The duplicity of this Apollinian covering over and unveiling may be implied in the curious fact that in "The Dionysian Worldview" (*1*, 560; cf. *1*, 36; 150) Nietzsche calls the Apollinian realm a *Mittelwelt*, an intermediary world; the word *Mittelwelt* points forward to what Nietzsche will envisage ten years later in the sailing ship, a *Mittelwesen* hovering between life and death, but also between male and female.

Dionysos lends his name to the rapturous states of intoxicated frenzy and the ecstasy of springtime. His is the world of sounds punctuated by intense, syncopated rhythms; of the transgression of outline, limit, and measure; of the *principium individuationis* in tatters. Here the artist himself or herself becomes the *work* of art, "the costliest marble." Yet here too we find a bewildering duplicity in play. Alongside the intense experience of *ecstasis* a peculiar kind of lucidity and deliberation (*Besonnenheit*) prevails. Yet how can such perspicuous perception accompany, without destroying, the work of art?

Each of these two duplicities involves a moment of insight or lucidity, *Erkenntnis* and *Besonnenheit*. Each implies a veiling or occluding that is seen as such. Each invokes a moment of imperturbable presence, presence as absolute propinquity. Nevertheless, these gods lend their names to distancings and removals, to transport beyond the horrific reality of existence and to seizure beyond all individuation. If we pursue the genealogies of these two gods, as Nietzsche himself traces them, we may learn more about the duplicity they share. A sharing that may help us mate them. So that we can finally see the mother.

Apollo is of course utterly Hellenic and Homeric in origin, even though the entire Homeric panoply rises in response to the wisdom of Silenus—the archaic Greek tutor of *Dionysos*. We recall the malevolent grin on the face of Silenus as he responds to his captor, King Midas, who demands to know what is best for man. Nietzsche's most dramatic transcription of Silenus' words appears in "The Birth of the Tragic Thought" (*1*, 588):

> Pathetic one-day brood of need and toil, wherefore do ye me violence that I might tell you what it would behoove you *not* to know? For in ignorance of your own misery you will pass your lives with least suffering. Once human you can never attain what is most praiseworthy and can never share in the essence of the best. The most excellent thing for all of you, taken singly and together, men as well as women, would be: not to have been born. But the next best thing once you have been born is: to die as soon as ever ye may!

The wisdom of Silenus becomes no more Hellenic when we hear it in the lilting language of W. B. Yeats's "From 'Oedipus at Colonus' ":

> Never to have lived is best, ancient writers say;
> Never to have drawn the breath of life, never to have looked into the eye of day;
> The second best's a gay goodnight and quickly turn away.

According to Nietzsche, the Apollinian dream-world of Olympus serves as a mirror by which the Hellenic world is able to confront an archaic, violent nature; confront and overcome it, subduing the Erinnyes, placating the Moirai, decapitating Medusa, arrogating the Gorgo. These figures, all of them female, provide our first cautious glimpse of the mother(s) of tragedy. Yet at a certain point in the history of Hellenism the Apollinian mirror cracks, the measure of the Apollinian style falters, and the gods on Olympus themselves grow livid at the wisdom of Silenus. Archaic violence stirs again, this time as an invasion from the mountains of Lydia. Nietzsche writes, after the manner of Hegel: " 'Excess' disclosed itself as truth" (*1*, 565). Enter Dionysos.

Although he has a savage Greek tutor, Dionysos (as Nietzsche knows him) is wholly Lydian, Asiatic, "oriental." His scepter is the ivy-wound *thyrsos*, his instrument the Pipes-of-Pan played in the Phrygian mode, *allegro molto vivace*. His other principal trait may be gathered from Nietzsche's references (in section 2 of *The Birth of Tragedy* and section 1 of "The Dionysian Worldview") to "the witches' brew of voluptuousness and cruelty," "pan-Hetaeric animal life," "the tiger and the monkey," and "the sexual promiscuity" of "Babylonian-Sekaean orgies." Second glimpse of the mother(s) of tragedy.

So foreign is oriental Dionysos to the Hellenic world that even after excess has disclosed itself as truth Dionysos must be domesticated. His music must be restrained in Apollinian cadences. The sexual release associated with his ὄργια must be transmuted into something quite different, something for which Nietzsche can find no Hellenic names but only Christian ones: he refers to "festivals of world redemption" and "days of transfiguration," *Welterlösungsfeste und Verklärungstage* (*1*, 32). The most astonishing gesture in this *rite de passage* for Dionysos occurs when Nietzsche's Apollo, playing the part of Pentheus in Euripides' *The Bacchae* (see l. 495), "removes the annihilating weapon from the hand" of the Lydian god (*1*, 32). If that weapon be the *thyrsos*, the phallic wand of Dionysos and his Maenad troupe, then the Lydian god is emasculated rather than domesticated. Unless of course Dionysos' association with all things female *before* his verge is taken from him makes him in some sense *always already* female? In which case: what would the weapon in Dionysos' hand be? Not merely the wand and cone, but also the ivy?[2]

This third glimpse of the mother of tragedy is perhaps most unsettling. Is a merely emasculated god capable of becoming the mother of tragedy? If the beating heart—what Hegel would call "the upswelling heart"—of Zagreus does not survive to be borne away and harbored in the godhead, how will tragedy be engendered? Yet what can it possibly mean to emasculate a preeminently feminine god, the god with down on his cheeks? What sort of distance opens here, at the instant of emasculation, such that both "masculine" and "feminine" traits are no longer fully present to our inspection and reflection, if indeed they ever were? We no longer dare skirt the issue. We must allow ourselves one final glimpse of the mothers. To be taken with exceeding care, lest they waken.

Nietzsche's most striking image of the fusion of Apollinian and Dionysian elements in tragedy, of radiant dream and lucid ecstasy, is a remarkable adaptation of a scene in Euripides' *The Bacchae* (ll. 664–774; cf. "The Birth of the Tragic Thought," *1*, 586–87). The Maenad throng, assembled on a mountain meadow at midday, have collapsed after their wild worship. In their sleep of exhaustion they dream. And what they dream is tragedy: reenactments of the fragmentation, rescue, restoration, and rebirth of the god. The oneiric rapture of these women, says Nietzsche, unites the qualities of extreme sensitivity and passionate suffering (*Leiden*) with "the most luminous contemplative nature and lucidity" (*1*, 591; cf. 31; 555–56; and 583). Such *Scharfsichtigkeit* and *Besonnenheit*, to be sure, will remain problematic throughout *The Birth*. What does it mean to want to bathe Dionysos in Apollinian light? To knock the weapon from the Lydian god's hand? Do these efforts aim to suppress or to acknowledge the god's feminine or bisexual nature? To repress or to release his/her sensuality as such? Are the incessant exchanges, communications, transports, dislocations, and proliferations of sensual love to give way to the stability and surety of pure presence, or must presence itself be postponed indefinitely?

That Nietzsche struggled relentlessly against the suppression and repression of difference and dislocation cannot be gainsaid. Ten years after the period we are discussing, in the notebook that introduces the first notes on eternal recurrence of the same, the following sentence (utterly devoid of context) appears: "Do not be one who despises voluptuousness!" (*9*, 547). Another five years later, four aphorisms from *Beyond Good and Evil* (numbers 155, 120, 75, and 141) show how intense the struggle would be, and how intimately the question of tragedy was to be touched by it:

> Sensitivity to the tragic increases and decreases in proportion with sensuality.

> Sensuality often overtakes the growth of love, so that the root remains weak and easy to tear out.

> A human being's degree and kind of sexuality reaches to the highest peaks of its spirit.

> Whatever is below the belt is the reason why human beings do not so readily take themselves to be gods.

Yet one need not advance fifteen years beyond *The Birth of Tragedy* to see the struggles, the inconsistencies, the loose ends. Nietzsche's early work urges us explicitly to take the way to the mothers (section 16), a way on which Dionysos alone can be our guide. Nietzsche nonetheless resists every step along that path. As befits a late Alexandrian, one who lives out the final turns of the Socratic supplement (sections 14–15), the young Nietzsche wants to *show* us Dionysos. We too, at the outer limit of that age when science bites its tail and recoils toward art, we too want to *see* how the meeting and mating of the gods takes place.

That the way to the mothers is fraught with peril is the lesson of Oedipus (section 9). For Oedipus attains the powers of insight and prophecy, the Apollinian *Einblick,* only after he has transcended the bounds of individuation through patricide, incest, and self-mutilation. In his notebooks Nietzsche associates the name *Oedipus* with two others—those of *Empedocles,* the philosopher of Love and Strife, and the music-practicing *Socrates*—in his search for "the tragic human being" who is in fact "the last philosopher." In the same notebooks (to which we shall now turn) Nietzsche has a great deal to say about *woman* in Greek antiquity.

Many sketches and plans of 1870–71 (see 7, 118, 124, 138, 158, and elsewhere) indicate a far more significant role for woman in *The Birth* than the role she eventually receives. In the book itself woman appears, as we have seen, in the formidable guise of Medusa. Her voluptuousness and cruelty, sensuality and cunning, are taken to be un-Hellenic, "oriental," "Asiatic." In contrast to the Hellenic myth of heroic Prometheus, the Hebrew myth of Sin and the Fall involves "curiosity, deceitful pretense, seducibility, lust— in short, a series of preeminently female affects. . . " (*1*, 69; 617). In a very real sense, Nietzsche's published writings reflect a world in which orientalism and the female ally to oppose everything Greek.[3] Even in the 1886 "Attempt at a Self-Criticism," where the question "What is Dionysian?" resounds, Nietzsche criticizes his early endeavors as "sugary . . . to the point of femininity" (*1*, 14). "Here something like a mystical and well-nigh Maenadic soul was speaking" (*1*, 15). The notebooks are more candid, less abashed.

I will say nothing here of the long notes on woman in the Greek polis (7, 143–48, 170–76, and elsewhere), except to note that the appearance of these passages in *The Birth* was postponed indefinitely. In general, they betray a remarkable ambiguity and ambivalence. While woman is for the Greeks a creature of the night, of solace and assuagement, "eternally the same," she is nonetheless the instigator of carnage and destruction: the Greek woman is Helen. Then again, woman is closer to nature and to god than is the male: the Maenadic sex supplies *Apollo* with his principal interpreters—the Pythia and Sibylla, Kassandra, Diotima, and Antigone (*1*, 42; 7, 137). Whereas Demeter and Dionysos remain outside the walls (7, 150–51), the priestesses of Apollo play a crucial role in the life of the city. It is Diotima (Plato, *Symposium* 201d) who holds in check for ten years the plague that eventually ravages Athens. Hence the "tragic philosopher" and "physician of culture" dare not ignore the question of woman. He must at all events take a stance "against the hatred of the body" (7, 542), especially the "young woman's body of the Sphinx" which "seduces us to existence" (7, 144); he must take a stance against the fear and hatred impacted in metaphysics since its inception. A note from early 1873 (7, 517) indicates that in this matter we cannot even identify the antiquity or modernity of the tragic philosopher:

> *The original purpose of philosophy has become futile.*
> Against iconic historiography.
> Philosophy, without culture, and science.
> Transformed position of philosophy since Kant.
> Metaphysics impossible. Self-castration.
>
> Tragic resignation; the end of philosophy.
> Only art can rescue us.

The tragic philosopher and physician of culture will have to confront problems that metaphysics itself has assiduously avoided throughout its history. In these notebooks (7, 149) Nietzsche cites the duplicity of the sexes— a duplicity that bewildered Kant—as one such problem.[4] A problem and a question here to be postponed, however, in order that we can confront Nietzsche's notes on the tragic philosopher of antiquity, the philosopher whose very postponements will be the pursuits of philosophers of the other dawn.

By way of prologue, an astonishing fragment from late 1872 (7, 460–61). Here the figure of Oedipus—through patricide, matrimony, and mutilation a figure of transgressions and transmutations—proves to be duplicitous in himself.

OEDIPUS
Talks
of the Last Philosopher
with Himself

A Fragment
from the History of Posterity

I call myself the last philosopher because I am the last human being. No one talks to me other than myself, and my voice comes to me as the voice of a dying man. With you, beloved voice, with you, the last vaporous remembrance of all human happiness, let me tarry just an hour more. With your help I shall deceive myself about my loneliness; I shall lie my way into society and love. For my heart

refuses to believe that love is dead, cannot bear the terror of the loneliest loneliness: it compels me to talk, as though I were two.

Do I hear you still, my voice? You whisper as you curse? And yet your curse
should cause the bowels of this world to burst! But the world lives on, gazing at
me all the more brilliantly and coldly with its pitiless stars; lives on, as brutish
and blind as it ever was; and only one dies—the human being. And yet! I hear
you still, beloved voice! Another besides me dies, another besides me, the last
human being in the universe: the last sigh, *your* sigh, dies with me—the prolonged *Woe! Woe!* sighed about me, the last of the men of woe, Oedipus.

The last human being, into whose "loneliest loneliness" will come in
ten years' time the demon whispering of eternal things, here undergoes a kind
of doubling. The "beloved voice" grows hushed, reducing to a whisper of
amor fati the curse that would annihilate the world. Oedipus the King attends
the queenly voice in him. The identification of the last human being as *Oedipus* is most wrenching, for it marks the end of antiquity; the identification of
him or her as the erotic *Socrates* is most seductive, dominating as it does our
own era; the identification of her or him as *Empedocles* is most disconcerting,
for it shows us our future.

In a school essay dated October 19, 1861, the seventeen-year-old
Nietzsche reports his first contact with Hölderlin's play, *The Death of Empedocles*. The epistolary essay ("A letter to my friend, in which I recommend
that he read my favorite poet") praises the "abundance of thought" and "supreme ideality" in Hölderlin, warmly recommending the poet's never-
completed tragedy: ". . . this remarkably significant dramatic fragment, in
whose melancholy tones resounds the future of the hapless poet, the living
grave of years spent insane; resounding not as you believe in nebulous chatter
but in the purest Sophoclean language and in an infinite richness of profound
thought."[5]

It is not difficult to discern why and how Hölderlin's *Der Tod des Empedokles* exercised such a strong influence on the young Nietzsche. For he was
already struggling—as contemporary essays and jottings of his show—to liberate himself from the oppressive constraints of his familial and cultural
heritage. The following sketch from Hölderlin's "Frankfurt Plan" for *The
Death of Empedocles*, the very first of such plans, exhibits the dramatic power
that the figure of Empedocles would come to exert on Nietzsche:

> Empedocles, by temperament and through his philosophy long since destined
> to despise his culture, to scorn all neatly circumscribed affairs and every interest
> directed to this or that object; an enemy to the death of all onesided existence,

and therefore also in truly beautiful relations unsatisfied, restive, troubled, simply because they are special kinds of relations felt solely in that magnificent accord with all living things which sates him utterly; simply because he cannot live in them and love them fervently with omnipresent heart, like a god, freely and expansively, like a god; simply because as soon as his heart and his thought embrace anything at hand he finds himself bound to the law of succession. . . . [6]

As Ritschl's student at Leipzig, Nietzsche later found independent access to Empedocles—through Diogenes Laertius and the fragments of Empedocles' poems. Whereas the importance of *Heraclitus* for the young Nietzsche is stressed on all sides, his fervor for Empedocles is obscured by the fact that *Philosophy in the Tragic Age of the Greeks* says so little about the Sicilian physician and magus. There are half-a-dozen references to Empedocles scattered throughout that incomplete treatise, all of them halcyon in tone; yet no discussion of his "marvelous poem" or staggering fate takes place. It is as though Nietzsche were postponing discussion of Empedocles till another time and place, perhaps for another kind of writing. For there are notes on Empedocles that could have inspired the very title *Philosophy in the Tragic Age of the Greeks*.

In the series of notes published in the Grossoktav and Schlechta editions as *Wissenschaft und Weisheit im Kampfe* (see the complete text in *8*, 97 ff.), Empedocles is omnipresent. The very first of Nietzsche's parallels between philosophy and music is "Empedocles-Tragedy [—] sacred monody" (*8*, 100). Empedocles is in fact the philosopher best suited to exemplify Nietzsche's own endeavors as a whole (*8*, 104): "My general task: to show how life, philosophy, and art can be related to one another in a more profound affinity, without the philosophy becoming banal or the philosopher's life dishonest." A long passage on Empedocles follows (*8*, 105; cf. 119):

> The *unsuccessful reformer* is **Empedocles**; when he failed, only Socrates was left. Aristotle's antipathy toward Empedocles is thus quite understandable.
> Empedocles—the sovereign state—alteration of a way of life—civil reform—an attempt made with the help of the great Hellenic festivals.
> Tragedy likewise was a means. Pindar?
> They did not find their philosophers and reformers; consider Plato, distracted by Socrates. Attempt to characterize Plato *without* Socrates. Tragedy—profound conception of love—pure nature—no fanatical renunciation—clearly, the Greeks were *about to find a still higher form of human being* than the prior forms; then came the scissors' cut. All we have is the *tragic age* of the Greeks.

What must be emphasized in these notes on Empedocles is the association of a profound conception of sexual love, "unadorned nature," with

Greek tragedy. Such an association is established in other notes and in Nietzsche's later published writings as well. [7]

After noting the emphasis on sexual passion and suffering in the early Greek poets, Nietzsche lists the philosophers and their salient traits: "Empedocles—blind love and blind hate; what is profoundly irrational in the world's most rational man" (8, 106). Such "irrationality" embraces the themes of Greek tragedy, but also touches on traditional philosophical problems such as *time*, conceived as *actio in distans*. For it is actually Empedoclean "love" and "hate" that instigate Nietzsche's notes (7, 571) on the ostensibly Pythagorean notion of "attraction, repulsion; affinity; *actio in distans.*"

Among the detailed notes on Empedocles there is one (23 [34] 1872–73; 7, 553–54) that deserves to be quoted in full. It explicates the relation of Empedoclean φιλία and Νεῖκος, love and hate as *actio in distans*, to sexual love (see also 8, 50 and 88):

> The symbolism of *sexual love*. Here, as in the Platonic fable, the longing for union manifests itself; we see that a greater unity once existed: if this greater unity were produced, it in turn would strive toward an even greater unity. The conviction that all living things are united testifies to the fact that there was once an *enormous living creature* of which we are fragments: it is of course the *Sphairos* itself. It is the most blessed divinity. Everything was bound by love alone; was thus supremely purposeful. Such love was torn and split asunder by enmity; was fractured in its element and thus killed, deprived of life. No living creatures rose within the vortex. Finally, everything was separated; and now our period begins. (He [Empedocles] contraposes to Anaxagoras' primal mixture a primal diremption.) Love, blind as it is, in raging haste tosses the elements together again, trying to bring them back to life. Here and there she succeeds. It goes on. A premonition rises in the animate creatures that they must strive toward still higher unifications as their homeland and primal condition. Eros. It is a frightful crime to take a life, for thus one strives backward in the direction of primal diremption. One day everything will again be one *single life*, the most blessed condition.
>
> The Pythagorean-Orphic doctrine in scientific transmutation: Empedocles consciously disposes over both means of expression, and is therefore the first *rhetor*. Political goals.
>
> Dual nature—the agonistic and the loving, compassionate.
> Attempt at *pan-Hellenic reform*.
>
> All anorganic matter originated from the organic; it is dead organic matter. Corpse and Man.

It is important to note that such dramatically Empedoclean thoughts—the preeminence of the organic, the "dual nature" of love and strife in nature, religion, and politics, and the erotic matrix of all these things—emerge once again ten years later in the notebook (M III 1) that contains Nietzsche's first jottings toward the thought of eternal return of the same. (See especially 9, 468 and 472-73.)

Before proceeding to Nietzsche's plans for the drama *Empedocles* we must take into consideration one last extended passage on that philosopher. In the following remarks, culled from the lectures on "The Pre-Platonic Philosophers" which Nietzsche delivered to his philology classes at Basel in 1872, 1873, and 1876, we find the clearest echoes of Nietzsche's postponed drama.[8]

The descendant "of an *agonal* family," Empedocles both in his person and in his doctrine appears at the acme of an entire tradition. His very appearance—the severe demeanor, the regal apparel—causes a sensation everywhere. Empedocles' task is to convert all the Hellenes to a rigorously Pythagorean way of life. Preaching the unity of all life, and prohibiting the eating of meat and various other foodstuffs, Empedocles elevates himself to the status of an immortal god. He transforms Parmenides' notion of the oneness of being into "the incomparably more productive" thought of the ἐν πνεῦμα, the unique soul of the world, the oneness of life. From this thought streams an intense feeling of pity or compassion for all living things—the very *Mitleidsgefühl* that will later prove to be Zarathustra's "gravest temptation." The task of human existence is thus

> to make good what νεῖκος has spoiled; to proclaim the thought of unity in love within the world of strife; and to be of aid oneself wherever suffering—the consequence of strife—is found. Heavy of heart, he wanders the world of travail, where all things are opposed. He can account for his presence in such a world only in terms of some sort of transgression: in some earlier epoch he must have committed some sacrilege, murder, or perjury. In such a world, guilt adheres to existence (XIX, 191).

Empedocles' teaching also exhibits a political dimension. Acragas finds itself on the crest of a wave of imperial splendor and luxury, yet is rent by the struggle between the new democracy, which Empedocles supports and even radicalizes, and the traditional tyranny. Here Empedocles' talents as rhetor unfold. After reforming the stormy politics of Acragas and rejecting the proffered crown, he travels throughout Greece. In Selinunt he quells a raging plague and is celebrated by the citizens as a god—an incident that will become central to Nietzsche's plans for an Empedoclean drama.

The *death* of this physician of culture also captures Nietzsche's imagination, as it had fascinated Arnold and Hölderlin before him. Empedocles' grave is never found, and legends abound concerning his transmutation into a god. His death is bound up with two events which, in somewhat altered form, will be important for Nietzsche's drama, namely, the reverence shown him by the citizens of plague-ridden Selinunt and the healing of the Acragan woman, Pantheia (see p. 111, n. 11, below). Among the sundry accounts of Empedocles' death, the "Ionian" version—his plunge into Etna—is the one that Nietzsche, following the lead of his forebears, will adopt.

A contemporary of Aeschylus, Empedocles is "the tragic philosopher" (XIX, 194). To him mortals seem to be castigated, fallen gods. "The earth is a gloomy cave, a malignant meadow, a λειμὼν ἄτης, where dwell murder, rancor, and a band of Keres such as illness and corruption" (ibid.). Every positive quality confronts an equally powerful opposite.

> In this world of conflict, suffering, and opposition, he finds only one principle that assures him of an altogether different cosmic order: he finds Aphrodite. Everyone knows her, yet no one discerns in her the cosmic principle . . . . Sexual life is in his view the best and noblest thing, the most stalwart opponent of the drive to diremption (XIX, 196).

The "best and noblest" drive, which Empedocles calls φιλία, has as its most intrinsic trait a "longing for the same," *die Sehnsucht zum Gleichen*. As such, the drive toward unification is an early emblem of eternal recurrence and its grand affirmation.

> Now, the properly Empedoclean thought is the *unity of everthing that loves*: it is *one* part of all things, compelling them to intercourse and unification. Yet there is also an inimical power that tears them apart. From their struggle results all coming to be and passing away. To be subjected to νεῖκος . . . is a terrible punishment. Transmigration through all the elements is a scientific appendage to Pythagorean metempsychosis: Empedocles himself asserts that he was once bird, bush, fish, boy and girl (ibid.)[9]

Although an Anaxagorean strain is visible in Empedocles' thought, Nietzsche stresses that this philosopher—as bird, bush, fish, boy and girl alike—had little enthusiasm for νοῦς. Pleasure and unpleasure, "the ultimate phenomena of life," sufficed. His was no mechanical universe of congealed beings jerked into motion by mind, but a cosmos of drives and animations, an ordered world without goals or purposes, a world in which each element coupled with all the others, a world in which chance was the only necessity. Nietzsche is perfectly aware of the resemblance of such a universe to that of Heraclitus (XIX, 200). He is also aware of its eminently tragic pathos. While Empedocles oscillates between science and magic, neither of these ever degenerates into a facile optimism; such oscillation earmarks Empedocles as a philosopher of the future, at the closure of the Socratic supplement.

> Empedocles remains forever on this *boundary*, and in almost all things he is a figure at the limits. He hovers somewhere between physician and sorcerer, poet and rhetor, god and human; between man of science and artist, statesman and priest; between Pythagoras and Democritus. He is the most colorful figure of ancient philosophy. Empedocles rings out the epoch of myth, tragedy, and orgiastics; yet in him appears the new Greek, as democratic statesman, orator, man of allegory and enlightenment, man of science. In him two epochs grapple with one another: he is through and through an *agonal* human being (XIX, 201).

Three clusters of plans and sketches in the notebooks of 1870-71 constitute the torso of Nietzsche's proposed drama, *Empedocles*. Only two of them will be important for us here, the third being no more than a draft of the play's opening (merely introductory) scene.[10] The earliest cluster originated some time between the autumn of 1870 and the first weeks of 1871 (*15*, 27-28). The first note of this cluster:

> 5 [116]†
> Act I. E [mpedocles] overthrows the [statue of] Pan, who refuses to answer him. He feels himself despised.
> The citizens of Acragas want to elect him King, an unheard-of honor. After a long struggle, he recognizes the delusion of religion.
> The most beautiful woman brings him the crown.
> II. Terrible plague; he organizes grand festivals, Dionysian Bacchanalia; art reveals itself as the prophetess of human woe. Woman as nature.
> III. He resolves while at a funeral ceremony to annihilate his people, in order to free them from their misery. Still more piteous to him are those who survive the plague.
> At the temple of Pan. "Great Pan is dead."

A number of familiar themes rise to meet us here: Plutarch's report of the death of Pan in *The Decline of the Oracles*, cited also in *The Birth of Tragedy*, section 11, and echoed in Nietzsche's hyperborean refrain, *Alle Götter müssen sterben* (*7*, 107 and 125); the citizens' proffering of the crown, an essential part of Hölderlin's play as well; the plague which in Nietzsche's estimation did much to bring the tragic age of the Greeks to a precipitous close. Yet what of this "most beautiful woman"? Of art as the "prophetess" of mortal misery? And of "woman as nature," *das Weib als die Natur?*

Ancient sources attest to the importance of an event in Empedocles' life involving a woman who was mortally ill. We shall soon see Nietzsche varying the theme of this woman, "Pantheia," for his own purposes.[11] The second fragment tells us more about Nietzsche's variation:

5 [117]†
The woman at the festival play rushes out and sees her lover fall to the ground. She wants to go to him. Empedocles holds her back and discovers his love for her. She relents, the dying man speaks; Empedocles is horrified by the nature that is revealed to him.

Empedocles is horrified by the nature that is disclosed to him in and through woman. What does the plague-stricken lover—for it is he and no longer Pantheia who collapses—tell Empedocles? What do his words have to do with the love Empedocles suddenly feels for the dying man's beloved?

The third and last fragment of the first cluster answers none of these questions, but it does tell us more about the hero of Nietzsche's tragic drama:

5 [118]†
Empedocles, compelled through all the stages, religion, art, science; bringing science to dissolution, he turns against himself.
Departure from religion, through the insight that it is deception.
Now joy in artistic semblance, driven from it by the recognized sufferings of the world. Woman as nature.
Now he observes the sufferings of the world like an anatomist, becomes *tyrannos*, uses religion and art, becomes steadily harder. He resolves to annihilate his people, because he has seen that they cannot be healed. The people are gathered about the crater: he grows mad, and before he vanishes proclaims the truth of rebirth. A friend dies with him.

"Bringing science to dissolution." Here it becomes clear that Nietzsche perceives Empedocles' situation as identical to his own—much in the way Matthew Arnold adjudges that situation typically "modern." Whereas Empedocles comes at the end of the first stirrings of science—a science which *Socrates* obviously cannot have introduced—Nietzsche comes at the end of the Alexandrian Age, when science is on the threshold of its final inversion to art—the supplement of Socrates-Mousikos. Empedocles too delights in the radiant semblance of Apollinian art. Yet such delight is subverted by the experience of Dionysian excess: the sufferings of the world embodied in "woman as nature." Nietzsche's theme is distinctly Faustian as well ("Departure from religion, through the insight . . . ," "Joy in artistic semblance . . . ," "Woman as nature . . . "), although significantly altered by Hölderlin's emphasis on the doctrine of rebirth. Finally, the reference to Empedocles' "becoming hard," his passion to annihilate, and his madness are disconcertingly prescient.[12]

The central cluster of *Empedocles* plans, composed no later than the autumn of 1872, and perhaps as early as the spring of 1871, is the most detailed and most revealing of the three. Not every word of these fragments need be reproduced here; yet a great deal is essential and merits more space than does any commentary. The first of these eight fragments:

8 [30]†
Greek memorial festival. Signs of collapse. Outbreak of plague. The Homeric rhapsode. Empedocles appears as a god in order to heal.
Infection with fear and pity. Antidote: tragedy. When one of the minor characters dies, the heroine tries to go to him. Enflamed, Empedocles holds her back; she grows ardent for him. Empedocles shudders before the face of nature.
The plague spreads.
Final day of the festival—sacrifice of Pan on Etna. Empedocles puts him to the test and obliterates him. The people flee. The heroine remains. In an excess of pity, Empedocles wants to die. He goes into the breach, managing to shout, "Flee!"—She: Empedocles! and then follows him. An animal rescues itself near them. Lava surrounds them.

Here tragedy rises as the *Gegenmittel* to fear and pity. Yet the antidote fails to contain the plague. The hero's infection with the very pestilence he wishes to cure foreshadows, as I have already noted, Zarathustra's ultimate temptation: pity for humankind. Yet what is the "test" to which Empedocles puts the great god of nature? Empedocles being the one who trembles to confront nature in a woman. Is *science* this test, a test that destroys the myths, then quails before nature's power? And what are we to make of the *sequence* of events, Empedocles "enflamed," the heroine aflame for him, he then recoiling with a shudder . . . . "The plague spreads." Why, when the citizens flee and Empedocles is left alone with the heroine, is the physician-philosopher overcome by pity and the miasmic dream of death? What is the animal they harbor in death? Could any living thing survive the lava?
The second fragment of the central cluster:

8 [31]†
An Apollinian god turns into a human being who craves death.
The strength of his pessimistic knowledge enrages him.
In an irruptive excess of pity, he can no longer bear existence.
He cannot heal the city, because it has degenerated too far below the Greek way to be.
He wants to heal it radically, namely, by destroying it; but here it salvages its Greek way to be.
In his godlike nature, he wants to help.
As a man, full of pity, he wants to annihilate.
As a daimon, he annihilates himself.
Ever more passionate waxes Empedocles.

Empedocles, a sort of *Mittelwesen* between Apollinian god and pitiful mortal, is driven to self-destruction. His trajectory is descensional, falling from incandescent god to creature consumed by compassion. Through neither religion nor science nor art can he alter the course of events in his city. His rage, pity, and passion engulf him.

Yet is it merely pity felt toward his corrupt and plague-ridden city that destroys him? The next fragment, which delineates the five acts of the tragedy, does not tell us; but the fourth begins by insisting that Empedocles "is free of fear and pity until the heroine's deed," that is, up to the moment she rushes to her stricken lover. If the fifth note communicates very little, the sixth and seventh at least tell us who this woman is. Her name is not Pantheia but Corinna.

Curt Paul Janz (I, 390) informs us that Corinna, who is present in neither Diogenes Laertius' *Lives* nor Hölderlin's *The Death of Empedocles*, is a historical figure. Corinna was a gifted Boeotian poetess. She tutored Pindar, and even defeated him in poetry competitions. We do not see her poetic talents in Nietzsche's plans, however: she may be the most beautiful of women; she is perhaps woman as nature, implicated in some dark way in plague and fatality; but her only word is "Empedocles!" Nevertheless, one must stress that in contrast to the anemic female characters of Hölderlin's three drafts, Nietzsche's Corinna plays a crucial role, a role that becomes clearer as the long eighth note elaborates the plot of this five-act tragedy.

8 [37]†

    I. Morning at twilight. [1.] Pausanias [i.e., the beloved pupil of Empedocles] bears a wreath to Corinna. The watchman tells of his [i.e., Empedocles'] appearances (Etna). 2. A group of country people arrive: a girl, fantasizing over Empedocles, suddenly dies. 3. Corinna sees the horrified Pausanias. Scene of assuagement. They reiterate their roles: on the verge of his major statement Pausanias grows taciturn and gloomy, cannot remember. 4. A plaintive procession, lyrical. 5. A scene among the people, fear of the plague. 6. The rhapsode. 7. Empedocles, with sacramental vessels; Pausanias in horror at his feet. The day grows bright. Corinna toward Empedocles.

    II. At the council. Empedocles veiled before an altar. The councilmen arrive one by one, cheerful, until each is affrighted by the veiled one. "The plague is in your midst! Be Greeks!" Fear and pity prohibited. Ludicrous scene in the council. Agitation among the people. The hall is taken by storm. The royal crown proffered. Empedocles orders the tragedy to be performed, consoles them on Etna, is revered. The tragedy is performed: Corinna's shudder.

    III. The Chorus.
        Pausanias and Corinna. Theseus and Ariadne.
        Empedocles and Corinna on stage.

Mortal turmoil among the people when rebirth is proclaimed. He is re-
vered as the god Dionysos, whereas he once again begins to feel pity. The
actor who is playing Dionysos ridiculously infatuated with Corinna.
The two murderers, who carry off the corpse. Raging lust for destruction
in Empedocles, enigmatically announced.
IV. Empedocles' proclamation concerning the coming evening's feast. Tur-
moil among the people, who feel secure because of their god's epiphany.
The elderly mother and Korinna.
Supreme calming effect.
In Corinna's house. Empedocles returns, gloomy.
V. Empedocles among his pupils.
Nocturnal celebration.
Mystic speech on pity. Annihilation of the drive to existence; death of
Pan.
Flight of the people. Two lava streams; they cannot escape! Empedocles
and Corinna. Empedocles feels like a murderer, deserving of unending
punishment; he hopes for a rebirth of penitential death. This drives him
to Etna. He wants to rescue Korinna. An animal approaches them. Ko-
rinna dies with him. "Does Dionysos flee in the face of Ariadne?"

No amount of commentary or speculation will banish the many mysteries here. Let me pose several questions, nevertheless.

What is the relationship between Pausanias and Corinna, that is, between the two objects of Empedocles' love? What is the wreath he brings her?
Is it his health? Is Pausanias the stricken lover of the earlier plans? And the
maiden whose fantasies on the hero are interrupted by her sudden death—
does she foreshadow Corinna's own fate? If so, why is Pausanias the one who
must be assuaged? What is the "principal statement" that never crosses his
lips? Is it the statement of the stricken lover, whispered earlier to Empedocles?

Again we note that fear and pity are the causes of plague, and that tragedy is to be the antidote. Yet how is the pity mentioned during the council
scene related to that inspired earlier by the heroine, her love and her fate?
And why the device of the tragedy within a tragedy? For all of Act III, under
the heading "The Chorus," proceeds as though the action described were the
dream of exhausted Maenads on a mountain meadow at midday.

And Corinna's shudder? Was it not Empedocles who shuddered earlier?
Is Corinna's shudder due to some impending conflict? If we may identify her
as Ariadne, is Pausanias then the mortal hero, Theseus? If so, then Empedocles himself, this "Apollinian god," would, at least on stage, become
Dionysos, "ridiculously infatuated"; Corinna would then be called upon to
choose between the mortal hero she has assuaged and the divinity she adores.

Yet another series of questions might be raised. Why does the proclamation of rebirth incite an ecstasy of death (*Todestaumel*) among the people? Are they not ready for it? As we shall see, this question will have to be raised again later, when it is a matter of *recurrence* rather than rebirth.

Meanwhile, Empedocles' counterpart, the stage-Dionysos, is mooning over Corinna. Have both the hero and the god been touched to the quick by this woman who is nature? The woman who is—we recognize her, yes, no mistake—the mother of tragedy?

Who are the two murderers, and who their corpse? Is it the duplicity of Empedocles-Dionysos, which has caused the sudden demise of one maid and will soon precipitate the fiery death of another? "Empedocles feels like a murderer," says the plan for Act V, after citing the couple, "Empedocles and Corinna." Is the doctrine of rebirth therefore proclaimed in the spirit of mortification, Empedocles being desirous of an infinity of penitential deaths? If it is, then we may have a sense of Empedocles' "mystic speech on pity," of his lust for destruction—the annihilation of the drive to existence.

Yet all the questions we might pose to the fifth and final act of the Empedoclean tragedy are in some way anticipated in the plan itself. For Nietzsche's plan ends with a question. A question placed in quotation marks, even though all the potential speakers have by now gone under. It is a question in scare quotes perhaps, posed to the tragedy as a whole. Indeed, we might wish to pick up the quotation gingerly by the hooks of these problematic marks and pose it as a question before and after *The Birth of Tragedy* and all its supplements.

"Flieht Dionysus vor Ariadne?"

Is it conceivable that the great god Dionysos, ostensibly accustomed to tugging mortals by their ears, is nonetheless all the while and without respite or assuagement fleeing flying bolting and retreating from or otherwise avoiding evading eluding shunning dodging not to say skirting his mate, whom all men without hesitation agree to call Ariadne? The mother of tragedy?

Pausanias, Empedocles, Corinna; Theseus, Dionysos, Ariadne. Hero, god, and mortal. The mortal in each case woman. The woman in each case nature. Nature in each case plagued. "And thus begins," writes Janz (I, 390), "the personal symbolism that was to accompany Nietzsche his whole life long, even into madness."

Head of Man below a Woman's Breast, ca. 1898–1908/09.
Woodcut. Oslo Kommunes Kunstsamlinger, Munch-museet.

CHAPTER THREE

Pana

I want to celebrate *reproduction* and *death* as a festival.

—From the plans to *Thus Spoke Zarathustra*, Part I (*10*, 138)

Have you whines for my wedding, did you bring bride and bedding, will you whoop for my deading is a? Wake?

—James Joyce, *Finnegans Wake*, I, 1

STUDY OF NIETZSCHE'S plans and sketches for the various stages of the book *Thus Spoke Zarathustra* corroborates what we have heard Karl Reinhardt suggest; namely, that the principal difficulty with the figure of Zarathustra is that he refuses to die, that is, to fulfill his tragic destiny. As I suggested earlier, it may well be that Heidegger's 1937 lecture course on Nietzsche, "The Eternal Recurrence of the Same," which asserts that Nietzsche never entertained any other notion concerning Zarathustra than *Untergang*, tragic downgoing, is a protracted response to Reinhardt's suspicion.[1] Not a little hangs in the balance: Nietzsche's principal thought and heaviest burden, eternal recurrence of the same, necessitates our looking into the question of Zarathustra's death, which, as we shall see, is postponed indefinitely. We will not be surprised to learn that this postponement has something to do with woman and sensuality. But before examining Nietzsche's unpublished sketches for a Zarathustran drama, sketches that are highly reminiscent of the abortive *Empedocles*, let us review briefly the sundry postponements of Zarathustra's death within *Thus Spoke Zarathustra*.[2]

That the book commences with downgoing has been universally noted: downgoing both as Zarathustra's mission (the teaching of overman) and as his demise (his collapse, convalescence, and postponed death). The entire book is caught in the tension and pull of "over" man, "down" going, and going "over": *Übermensch, Untergang, Übergang*. The meaning of the *über* is itself bifurcated along vertical and horizontal axes. *Übermensch* is somehow *above* mankind and *beyond* human history; *Übergang* is a crossing *over* or going *across* the bridge of the future to a new kind of humanity. No wonder commentators today are wrestling with the problem of the relation between historical mankind and overman! For the ambiguity, the double axis of the project, is ineluctable and irreducible.[3] Such ambiguity marks the task of descensional thinking as such—the problem as to *how* Zarathustra is to go down and under.[4] *Thus Spoke Zarathustra* commences with downgoing. Each of its four parts tries to *end* with downgoing. Tries but fails. Postpones the *Untergang*.

Even after the tightrope walker has shown Zarathustra the way down, Nietzsche's hero beguiles himself with false goals. By the end of the Prologue he has adopted the speech and the mannerisms of the practical joker, the actor, the gravedigger. Indeed, a note from the year 1883 explicitly identifies Zarathustra as the *Possenreisser* (*10*, 531). "Let my going be their downgoing!" he cries (*4*, 27), already oblivious of the downgoing that can only be his own.

The penultimate episode of Part I, "On Free Death," an episode to which Heidegger will not be blind,[5] envisages Zarathustra's own death. Envisages it and then executes it by ruse, as it were, suddenly introducing the imperfect tense into Zarathustra's speech, as though the downgoing were already accomplished. Envisages, executes, and then postpones it by means of an untranslatable pun. As follows:

> Thus I myself want to die, so that you friends will love the earth all the more for my sake; and I want to become earth again, so that I find rest in her who bore me.
>
> Truly, Zarathustra had a goal; he tossed his ball. Now you friends are the inheritors of my goal: I toss the golden ball to you.
>
> More than anything, my friends, I want to see you tossing the golden ball! And so I linger a bit longer on earth: forgive my malingering! [*Und so verziehe ich noch ein Wenig auf Erden: verzeiht es mir!*]

In the final episode of Part I, "On the Gift-giving Virtue," Zarathustra reminds his disciples to remain "true to the earth." He then cautions them to be chary of him. "And better still: be ashamed of him! Perhaps he betrayed you" (*4*, 101). At "Midday," in Part IV, hundreds of pages later, Zarathustra is still tossing that ball (see *4*, 344), still malingering.

Part II begins with announcements of Zarathustra's pregnancy (with the doctrine of overman) and ends with Zarathustra's "stillest hour." The latter Zarathustra calls his "terrifying mistress," the mistress of his loneliness. She utters the voiceless cry, "What do you matter, Zarathustra? Speak your word and shatter!" (*4*, 188). Yet Zarathustra does not deliver, does not collapse; again he goes to embrace his solitude.

The postponements of Part III are considerably more complex. Perhaps all of them devolve upon the curious fact that in the original manuscript the second episode, "On the Vision and the Riddle," is set *within* the narrative frame of the much later episode, "The Convalescent." Nietzsche originally began "On the Vision and the Riddle" with the sentence (crossed out at the proof-stage), "But what is it I dreamt not long ago as I lay on my sickbed?" (*14*, 309). The suggestion is that the vision (the glance of an eye, or moment of time) and the riddle (the shepherd writhing in nausea) are intrinsic to con-valescence itself; they are not illnesses that one might leave behind, maladies from which one might totally convalesce. Indeed, what would it mean to convalesce from the moment of time? Surely one would then owe a cock to Aesclepius? At all events, the longing that Zarathustra experiences at the end of the riddle, when he hears the shepherd's golden laughter, induces the dream of death: "My longing for this laughter gnaws at me: Oh, how can I bear to go on living! And how I could bear now to die!" (4, 202). Yet in the episode "The Convalescent," near the end of Part III, Zarathustra's animals beg him not to die; they transform the burden of eternal recurrence into a ditty that promises immortality. They now speak in Zarathustra's name, ar-rogate his voice, proclaim the "end" of his downgoing as such.

> "Now I dwindle and die," you would say, "and in a nonce I'll be nought. Souls are as mortal as bodies.
> "But the knot of causes that binds me recurs—it will create me again! I my-self belong among the causes of eternal return.
> "I shall come again, with this sun, with this earth, with this eagle, with this serpent—*not* to a new or better or similar life:
> "I shall come again to this selfsame life, identical in its grandest and small-est details, so that again I shall teach the eternal return of all things. . . .
> "I spoke my word, I shatter on my word. Thus my eternal lot wills it: as one who announces, I perish!
> "The hour now has come for the downgoer to bless himself. Thus—*ends* Zarathustra's downgoing."

Meanwhile, Zarathustra hears nothing of the words his animals would put into his mouth—for the sighs of Oedipus have now become the musings of Zarathustra's animals. He lies still, "communing with his soul." In the original manuscript, as we know, his "soul" bears the name *Ariadne*. The epi-sode that tells of his communing, "On the Great Longing," preserves a num-ber of allusions to Ariadne: hers is the vine heavy with golden grapes hanging in clusters like udders (see *4, 279, 401*; and *10, 447*). Her wine is a whine (*Wein-Weinen*), a lament or complaint (*Klage-Anklage*). And the imagery suddenly becomes ambiguous as the overripe soul begs for the vintner's knife: "In flowing tears pours out all your suffering, your suffering from abundance and from the cluster's urge to go to the vintner and the vintner's knife!" (4, 280). A note from the summer of 1883 fashions a similar image, although Zarathustra's soul here exhibits a new name (10, 447): "And what shall I do with your knife, Pana? Shall I sever the yellow grapes from the vine? Behold, what abundance surrounds me!"

Traces of Ariadne persist in the following episode of Part III, "The Other

Dance Song," originally entitled "*Vita Femina.*" "I dance after you, I follow you along the barest trace," says Zarathustra (*4*, 283), as though he were Theseus. Or Dionysos. For life, as we soon learn, has "delicate ears." Yet in the "Seven Seals, or Yes and Amen Song," Zarathustra appears to spurn life, growing "ardent for eternity." "Never yet have I found the woman from whom I want children, unless it be this woman, whom I love: for I love you, O Eternity!" (*4*, 287).[6] It is not clear how Zarathustra's ardor for eternity will conform to his tragic fate. Unless he and we stop our ears to the animals' ditty and return to the *gateway* of eternity, the portal of time and mortality.

In the fourth part of *Thus Spoke Zarathustra* a hoary Zarathustra announces that he is still not ready, that there is still time to go under (*4*, 297). Not that *Untergang* can be postponed forever (*4*, 298):

> But I and my destiny—we are not appointed for today, though also not for never: we have time and overtime for our talk. For one day he must surely come, he dare not pass me by.

Yet the "high dramatic tension" of this fourth and final part is sustained, not by Zarathustra's approaching destiny, but by his ceaseless, bootless search for the Higher Men. The latter, Zarathustra's sundry shadows, are all ultimately rejected—even the "ugliest man," who clearly achieves the affirmative thought of eternal recurrence (*4*, 396). Rejected in order that Zarathustra can perpetuate his search and so lay claim to a new morning: "Thus spoke Zarathustra, and stepped out of his cave, glowing and strong, like a morning sun emerging from dark mountains. —End of *Thus Spoke Zarathustra*" (*4*, 408). How differently Nietzsche's classic work would have resounded if Nietzsche had adopted for it an ending he had sketched during the winter of 1884–85, and if he had altered the final episodes of Part IV to attune them to that ending (31 [20][†]; *11*, 365):

> Thus Zarathustra rose like a morning sun emerging from the mountains: glowing and strong he strode forward—off to the magnificent midday which his will craved, and descending to his downgoing.

Do these postponements of Zarathustra's demise have anything to do with the postponements examined earlier, those having to do with sensual love and woman? Among the notes from July through August of 1882, that is, from the period of *The Gay Science*, we find references to sexuality and death as the two fundamental themes of Nietzsche's projected book *Plowshare*. The ninth point of a ten-point plan (*10*, 21) raises the question of the " 'Preservation of the species' and the thought of eternal return." The first five points read:

1. Dissatisfaction with ourselves. . . .
2. To transform the figure of death as a means of victory and triumph.
3. Sexual love as a means toward an ideal (Striving to go down in one's opposite.) Love for the suffering godhead.
4. Illness, our behavior toward it, Freedom unto Death.
5. Procreation as the holiest matter. Pregnancy, creation by the woman and the man who want to enjoy in the child their *unity* and who want to erect a *monument to that unity.*

The same notebook contains a detailed plan on the question of woman (*10*, 24–25). Its final point: "Sensuality different in man and woman." When Nietzsche recopied these notes into the "Tautenburg Sketches for Lou von Salomé" (*10*, 42), he dropped this final point. Yet earlier in the sketches we find (*10*, 37): "*Love* is, for *men*, something altogether different than it is for women. For most men, love is of course a sort of possessiveness [*Habsucht*]; for others, love is adoration of a suffering and veiled godhead."

The interlaced themes of sensual love and death emerge much more clearly from the plans for Part II of *Thus Spoke Zarathustra* (summer, 1883). Here we find a number of startling reminiscences of the *Empedocles* plans sketched a dozen years earlier. Here the very same problem arises out of the matter or "stuff" of *Zarathustra*. Like Empedocles, Zarathustra is searching for his tragic destiny. He has a mission, yet must learn to interweave mission and fate. His speeches in Part I have failed to fulfill that destiny. Looking forward to Part II, Nietzsche jots one such reminiscence of Empedocles (*10*, 366):

Conversation with the *hound of hell.*
(Vulcan)
Over ashes I stride, up the cindered mountain at eventide: my shadow grows longer and longer.
A bark drifts in the distant violet sea: the seaman who sees me stride crosses himself.
"Now Zarathustra voyages to hell," he says with a shudder. "Long ago I foresaw that this would be his end!"
"Wrong you are, fisherman, altogether wrong! The devil isn't fetching me: it's Zarathustra who is fetching the devil."

Zarathustra's conversation with the hound of hell preserves its Empedoclean *setting* in *Thus Spoke Zarathustra*, Part II. Indeed, there may be grounds for identifying the city of Motley Cow with ancient Acragas, and Zarathustra's island habitat as Sicily. Be that as it may, the episode "On Great Events" (*4*, 167–71; cf. *10*, 373) begins as follows:

There is an island in the sea—not far from Zarathustra's Blessed Isles—on which a volcano constantly belches out its smoke. The people there say (and it is mainly the old women who say it) that it was placed there like a boulder before the portal of the underworld, but that a narrow path through the volcano itself leads to this very portal.

However, the hound of hell who guards the portal turns out to be a yapping "fire dog": a potentially Empedoclean destiny for Zarathustra dwindles to a chastisement for socialists and anarchists.

Nevertheless, the theme of Zarathustra's death is not so readily quashed. We soon find in the notebooks, underlined several times, directions for Zarathustra's "last speech," and nearby the following "prophecy" (*10*, 372):

> One day I shall have my summer: and it will be a summer as in the high mountains.
> A summer near the snow, near the eagle, near death.

Hard upon the prophecy appear the first plans for a Zarathustran *drama*, in which death—though not yet woman—plays a crucial role. The final three notes of N VI 3, from June through July of 1883, read as follows (*10*, 377–78):

> 10 [45]†
> Act I. The temptations. He feels he is not yet ripe. (Selected people)
> *Loneliness arising from his own shame*
> Act II. Zarathustra attends incognito the "magnificent midday"
> Is recognized
> Act III. Catastrophe: *everyone* turns away after *his* speech.
> He dies from the pain.
> Act IV. Obsequies
> "We killed him"
> **Persuades the reasons**
>
> 10 [46]†
> For Act I. He refuses. In the end, in tears because of the children's choruses.
> A *jester*!
> 2 Kings lead the donkey.
> For Act II. When the procession does not know which way to turn, the emissaries arrive from the city of the plague. Decision. As in the *forest*. Fire in the marketplace, symbolic purification.
> Annihilation of the *metropolis* the end
> I want to seduce the *pious*.
>
> 10 [47]†
> Zarathustra sitting on the ruins of a church   Act IV
> *the mildest one must become hardest—and thereby perish*

Mild toward humanity, hard for the sake of overman
Collision.
apparent *weakness*.
he prophesies to them: the doctrine of recurrence is the *sign*.
He **forgets himself** and teaches recurrence **on the basis of** *overman*: overman *withstands it* and *disciplines by means of it*.
When he returns from his vision he dies on account of it

Nothing about these plans is obvious or entirely straightforward. The
"temptations" of Act I refer to Zarathustra's shame and pity, virtues (that is,
vices) he must learn to outstrip. As we shall see in the next chapter, the very
last *Zarathustra* plans invoke the same *Versuchungen*. Zarathustra's "selected
people," a parody of the "Chosen," are the Higher Men, the bridges to the
future that is overman. "Magnificent midday" is the moment when Zarathustra communicates his most burdensome thought, thus precipitating a
crisis or "catastrophe" for those who cannot bear eternal recurrence. Yet in
these plans catastrophe strikes Zarathustra himself, who dies of grief and dis-
appointment. The plaint of those who reject him, "We killed him," recalls
the cry of the madman in *The Gay Science* (number 125) who proclaims the
death of God (3, 480–82). The obsequies (*Leichenfeier*) mentioned here find
their echo in the wake (*Totenfeier*) portrayed in subsequent plans (*10*, 379–
82); yet as the plans proceed it becomes clear that the wake will not be Zarathustra's, insofar as his death will have been postponed indefinitely.

The role of the jester in the second plan is unclear, even though he appears more than once in the notebooks (cf. *10*, 382); the two Kings and their
donkey are unmistakable foreshadowings of the fourth part of *Thus Spoke
Zarathustra* (4, 304). The plague-ridden city (*Peststadt*) is transported directly from the pages of the *Empedocles* plans of 1870–71. "The forest" may
be the habitat of the pious old saint in Zarathustra's Prologue. It is mentioned
in later notes (e.g., *10*, 415 and 583) and will eventually become the pri-
meval forest or jungle of the final plans for *Zarathustra*.

The third plan introduces a strange ambiguity into the drama plans:
whereas Act IV in the first note has our hero lying in state, the commentary
has him perched on the ruins of a church! The dilemma of the Zarathustra-
type is nonetheless clearly stated: the necessity of Zarathustra's "becoming
hard" will reverberate throughout plans to the third and fourth parts of *Thus
Spoke Zarathustra*, and this rigorous project will serve to keep Zarathustra
alive. The "collision" stressed here is surely the catastrophe that occurs when
Zarathustra teaches the doctrine of eternal return before its time: the doctrine is itself intended for overman, who alone can endure it. Yet in this third

plan it is not a matter of the *others* turning away or of Zarathustra's death from grief: here Zarathustra dies because he has trespassed onto the ground of over-man, a ground he does not command, so that the vision of eternal recurrence becomes (or should become) his own final, irrevocable *Untergang*.

As we approach the next plan for a Zarathustran drama in Nietzsche's notebooks, a number of pertinent yet disjointed notes rise to meet us as echoes of "Zarathustra's holy laughter." Here again (*10*, 442) are fragments of Zarathustra's "last speech," citing pity as the danger for overman and downgoing as Zarathustra's destiny ("But it is my felicity now to go down"). Suddenly a woman's voice is heard (*10*, 443[†]), as though hers were the voice of Zarathustra himself: " 'Thus I gladly die! And die countless times more! And live in order thus to die!' And as she died she smiled: for she loved Zarathustra." The following four notes (ibid.[†]) invoke "catastrophe," and introduce the woman herself. Which woman? The second and fourth notes betray her identity, if not her name.

> A storm growls in the sky, not yet visible.
> Then a crack of thunder, followed by stillness—as though in frightful coils this stillness wrapped us round and bound us: the world stood still.

> Then the woman announces the coming of eagle and serpent. The sign. Universal flight. The plague.

> She drew Zarathustra's arm to her breast.

> And again the abyss breathed: it groaned and roared its fire forth.

We know that the woman is Corinna, herself a shadow of Ariadne, whatever she will call herself now. The next detailed drama plan appears, still among notes for Part II of *Thus Spoke Zarathustra* (*10*, 444–45):

13 [2][†]
Act I. Zarathustra among animals. The cave.
  The child with the mirror. (It is time!)
  The various queries, tension mounting. Finally, the children seduce him with song.
Act II. The city, outbreak of plague. Zarathustra's procession, the healing of the woman. Springtime.
Act III. Midday and Eternity.
Act IV. The sailors.
  Scene on the volcano, Zarathustra *dying among children*.
  The wake.

Auguries.
For Act III: Zarathustra saw and heard nothing, he was enchanted.

Then gradually his most frightful knowledge returns. The indignation of his disciples, abandonment by his favorites, Zarathustra tries to hold them. The serpent lashes its tongue at him. He recants, excess of pity, the eagle flees. Now the scene with the woman, in whom once again the plague irrupts. Out of pity he kills her. He embraces the corpse.

Then the ship and the appearance on the volcano. "Zarathustra is going to hell? Or does he want to redeem the underworld now?" —Thus the rumor spreads that he is also the Wicked One.

Final scene on the volcano. Full of beatitude. Oblivion. Vision of the woman (or of the child with the mirror) The disciples gaze into the deep grave. (Or *Zarathustra among* **children** at the temple ruins.)

The grandest of all wakes constitutes the conclusion. Golden sarcophagus is plunged into the volcano.

We recognize the child with the mirror from the first episode of *Zarathustra*, Part II. And the sailors observing the volcano we know from the episode "On Great Events." Yet in that episode, as I have already noted, the impressive backdrop to the Empedoclean and Zarathustran tragedies seems overdrawn and out of place, inasmuch as it becomes the scene of yet another speech. Zarathustra's death among children, amid the ruins of a temple, reminds us of Nietzsche's Heraclitean heritage, of the universe in which play is king; his plunge into the volcano that towers over the plague-ridden city is however altogether Empedoclean.

The crucial act involves several elements: the betrayal by Zarathustra's animals, the flight of his pride; his excess of pity for the Higher Men, disciples who are not yet ready for his teaching; and the woman who embodies love (as the corpse which Zarathustra in his folly embraces) and plague (which again breaks out in her, *an dem wieder die Pest ausbricht*). Only a kind of sacrificial killing (cf. *10*, 152: *der heilige Mord*) will heal her. And perhaps not even that: is she not still a source of infection when Zarathustra embraces her? Whatever the case, it is but a moment from that embrace to "the most magnificent of wakes" and the plunge of Zarathustra's coffin into the crater.

The moment of betrayal by the animals (or the moment when their fidelity becomes lethal), a moment that is utterly foreign to *Thus Spoke Zarathustra* as we know it, receives elaboration in two further notes (*10*, 446–47[†] and 513[†]), from the summer and autumn of 1883:

> But when he saw the serpent lashing its tongue at him his face slowly, slowly changed: the door of his knowledge sprung open in spite of all he could do: like lightning it struck into the depths of his eyes, and, once again, like lightning; only a moment more and he would have known— —When the woman saw this transformation she screamed as though in extreme distress: "Zarathustra, die"—

> With his left hand he fended off the eagle, who battered him with a wild flurry of wings, screeching as though to urge flight; the eagle would gladly have carried him off. To his right, on the table, the tablet of stone

And several months later:

> When they have all gone, Zarathustra stretches his hand toward the serpent: "What does my discernment advise me?" The serpent lashes out at him. The eagle tears the serpent to shreds, the lion pounces on the eagle. When Zarathustra saw the struggle among his animals, he died.

The woman who cries out in distress, who in an excess of pity calls for Zarathustra's death, is presumably the very woman Zarathustra himself murders out of pity—although the interchangeable roles and sexes ought to give us pause. She is no longer called Corinna, but Pana, and she is designated in several notes from this period.[7] The first note (*10*, 446[†]):

> "But you know it, Pana, my child, my little star, my ear of gold—you know that I love you too?"
> Your love for me has persuaded you, I can see it: but I still do not understand the will of your love, Pana!—

The second note (*10*, 447[†]) we have seen already in the context of "[Ariadne:] The Great Longing":

> "And what shall I do with your knife, Pana? Shall I sever the yellow grapes from the vine? Behold, what abundance surrounds me!"

By this time, it is impossible to tell who is wielding the knife against whom, as when Quentin Compson threatens Caddy and himself in *The Sound and the Fury* ("it wont take but a second just a second then I can do mine I can do mine then"). The third note proceeds to confound the two thoroughly (*10*, 512[†]):

> When he recognizes Pana, Zarathustra dies out of pity for her pity. Prior to that, the moment of great contempt (supreme felicity!)
> Everything must come to fulfillment; namely, everything in the *Prologue*.

It is difficult to know what Nietzsche means by "everything in the *Prologue*," although one might expect Zarathustra's irrecoverable *Untergang* to be among those things. And now his downgoing is bound to the fatality called *Pana*. Indeed, the two figures are nearly identical; the smallest gap separates them. That gap is marked by the parentheses in the phrase "the moment of great contempt (supreme felicity!)." The smallest gap (*10*, 437[†] and 449[†] [cf. 366]):

> I do not touch her soul: and soon I shall no longer even reach her skin. The last, smallest gap is most difficult to bridge. Did I not hurt you all most when I was kindest to myself?

> Now only the smallest gap stands between me and you: but woe! who was ever able to span a bridge across the smallest gaps?

Because of Heidegger's interpretation we are accustomed to think of the smallest gap in terms of the distance between Zarathustra's thinking of eternal recurrence and the caricatures of that doctrine produced by the spirit of gravity and Zarathustra's animals.[8] How disconcerting to have to think of the rainbow and the asses' bridge as links to Pana!

Later notes (*10*, 468) seem to reduce the figure of Pana to one of piety: she who cries "Zarathustra, die!" is transformed into one of those "pious ones" cited in an earlier plan who are ripe for seduction. Or to a figure of comedy (*10*, 469): the woman Zarathustra murders responds in religious puns: "How well you heal, O healing Savior!" Furthermore, these later plans (*10*, 471–73) remove "the wake" from its position of climax in the drama of Part II; and, as we know, the published text of *Thus Spoke Zarathustra* contains no *Totenfeier*, certainly none featuring Zarathustra himself. Plans for Part III do continue to call for Zarathustra's demise: "In the last speech the *Grave Song* too must be **fulfilled!**" (*10*, 480). Yet that demise is deferred by calls for Zarathustra to become "legislator," calls that begin to resound here and that grow more and more clamorous until the notebooks are suddenly blank.

In the autumn of 1883 a third cluster of plans for a Zarathustran drama crystallizes—two of its notes we have cited already. The principal plan follows an important statement concerning the impact of the thought of eternal return (*10*, 495–96):

16 [3] †
    In Act II the various groups come, bearing their gifts. "What did you do?"—They tell him.—"Then you have done it in the spirit of Zarathustra."
    At first the riffraff will smile on the doctrine of return, for they are cold and without much inner need. The most vulgar drive to life is the first to grant its consent. **A great truth always wins over to itself the highest human beings last**: this is what everything true must suffer.
    Act I. Loneliness arising from his own shame: *an unexpressed thought, for which he feels too weak (not hard enough) The temptations to deceive himself about this.* Emissaries from the Selected People invite him to the feast of life.
    Act II. He attends the feast incognito. He betrays himself, feeling that they show him too much reverence.
    Act III. In a state of euphoria he proclaims the overman and his doctrine. Everyone turns away. He dies when the vision abandons him and he sees, with great pain, the suffering he has caused.
    The Wake. "We killed him"—Midday and Eternity.

The resemblance to the first drama plan is evident, although here the religious parody is more pronounced. Central to this plan is the incommunicability of eternal return, or at least the fatality of premature communication. Another note in the same series warns (*10, 520*), "N.B.: *The thought itself will not be expressed in the third part*: merely prepared. First of all, *critique of everything taught heretofore.*" Part III of *Thus Spoke Zarathustra* does communicate the thought of return, but only in altercations with the dwarf and the animals, always masked and encrypted, always across the smallest gap. The dramatic import of Zarathustra's shame begins to be felt now, his feeling of weakness in the face of his own teaching, his awareness of the likelihood of self-deception. We recall that the salient characteristic of *Dionysos philosophos*, to whom Nietzsche will soon turn, is his *lack* of shame.

However, the drama now reverts to its initial form, abandoning its female personage and the theme of plague. The emissaries of Zarathustra's "Selected People" now invite him to celebrate life. Here there is no call for heroic decision. Here no Pana threatens him with her pity, her piety, or her knife. Here there is no womanly nature to kill or be killed by.

If she shrinks to piety before disappearing altogether from the drama, it nonetheless will not do to forget that Pana entered on the scene wearing the mask of Ariadne. Pan-a is the mate, if not of Dionysos, then of the great god Pan, with whom Empedocles contended on Etna. She is perhaps the universe of nature herself (τὸ πᾶν), plurality and diversity in the flesh. Perhaps her name reflects Nietzsche's passion to demythologize, to cross out the reference to divinity: Pan-~~the~~-a. Whatever the case, Pana's story is now postponed, the feast of life celebrated without her. And without the pestilence.[9]

Yet Zarathustra manages for a time to meet in these plans his tragic destiny without her aid. As though the place and function of Pana are now occupied and performed by the thinking of eternal recurrence itself. Zarathustra's euphoria now betrays him, induces him to speak out of turn. The havoc his words wreak among the Last Humans, who can only gnash their teeth at the thought of return, occasions Zarathustra's gravest temptation: his pity for humankind. "Midday and Eternity," a title that becomes ever more prominent during the last years of Nietzsche's active life, is now transferred from the third to the fourth act, from the announcement of return to "the wake" itself. The wake is now without an act designated especially for it, as though it were on its way out. In the remaining *Zarathustra* plans, for Parts III and IV, the tension waxes between two poles; that is, between Zarathustra's task to become hard, to overcome shame and pity, to teach recurrence, and Zarathustra's tragic destiny, to go down to human beings, to speak his word and shatter, to make way for the overman. The tension does not subside. If some notes insist on the "**transition from the free spirit** and hermit to the *necessity to* **dominate**" (*10*, 516; cf. 532, 542), others expose the vulnerability of the Zarathustra-type itself (*10*, 500 and 517):

> That Zarathustra achieves his supreme *need* and only thereby his supreme *fortune*: step-by-step he becomes less happy *and* more fortunate.
> At the moment when both stand in most horrific contrast to one another, he perishes. . . .

> The *group* who make sacrifice on Zarathustra's *grave*: formerly they had fled: now that they find him dead they become the *legatees* of his soul, and they are elevated to **his height**. (This last scene in Zarathustra 4—"Magnificent Midday—cloudless—azure sky)

The same tension lends form to the final cluster of plans. The work is no longer conceived as a drama, although the plans still show signs of their dramatic provenance. Indeed, there are grounds for saying that Part IV of *Thus Spoke Zarathustra* is the most "dramatic" of the four books, the one in which actions finally speak louder than words—as they did in the Prologue—and in which deeds and omissions stretch across the entire expanse of the text. The first of these final plans (see *10*, 518[†]) reads:

Plan for Zarathustra 4.
1. The victory procession, the plague-ridden city, the symbolic heap of ruins. 30[10]
2. Annunciations of the future: his pupils recount *their deeds.* 30
3. The final speeches with auguries, interruptions, rain, death. 30
4. The group at his grave—the oath-takers—magnificent midday—full of *premonitions, serene* and *spine-tingling.* 30

The question we might pose to this plan—and Nietzsche himself poses it (*10*, 519)—is whether Zarathustra "finally grasps the fact" that it is not enough to teach recurrence; that one must "also *forcefully change* the human beings who adopt" the teaching. The oath-takers at Zarathustra's gravesite (who are mentioned also in later plans for a book to be entitled *The Eternal Return;* see *11*, 10) themselves testify to the fact that Zarathustra fails to grasp it. Further plans interpret the notion of self-overcoming as implying Zarathustra's withdrawal from the scene in favor of overman (*10*, 522–23[†]):

> The third part[11] is the self-overcoming of Zarathustra, as *prototype* of the self-overcoming of humanity—on behalf of the overman.
> For *that* the overcoming of morality is necessary.
> *You sacrifice your friends*—they are deep enough to perish on account of it: and they did not create the thought (my having created it still sustains *me!*)
> This as the final counterargument Zarathustra poses to himself—his strongest *enemy. Now Zarathustra ripens.*

In Part 4 Zarathustra dies when he observes his friends' misery: and when they abandon him. —But after his death his spirit comes over them. . . .

At the same time, other fragments of plans (*10*, 525–26) imply that Zarathustra has all the time in the world, that he is tranquil and unperturbed. Far from plunging headlong to hell, Zarathustra enjoys recuperation and convalescence. After which he "stands there like **Caesar**." And not on the Ides of March. It becomes clear that the plague and the wake will be deflected in such a way that Zarathustra himself *carries* the former and *attends* the latter (see, for example, *10*, 559–60, 591–92, and 611).

Yet Zarathustra's convalescence applies only to the plans for Part III. Zarathustra's death and the plague of Pana have once again merely been postponed. Some extracts from a detailed plan for Part IV of *Thus Spoke Zarathustra*, drawn up in the autumn of 1883 (*10*, 593–94):

20[10] [†]

. . . Zarathustra describes ever-smaller circles: long speeches in which he *excludes*. Ever-smaller circles, on ever-higher mountains. . . .

Last scene: portrayal of the *highest souls*, who can run deepest; those with the greatest range, who can go farthest astray; the most necessary, who plunge into hazards; beings that fall in love with becoming; . . . those for whom all is play . . . , the world a god's jubilation. . . .

All creatures mere **preliminary exercises** in the *unification* **incorporation** *of opposites*. . . .

Then Zarathustra, *on the crest of the euphoria of the overman*, relates the **secret** that everything recurs.

Impact. Pana wants to kill him.

Finally he grasps it, proceeds through all the metamorphoses, to the most victorious one; but when he sees her lying there, shattered, he—*laughs*. Laughing, he ascends the mountain crag: arriving there, he dies a happy death.

Tremendous impact of his *death*: the oath-takers.

Once again Pana wields the knife; once again, by a kind of doubling or reversal, she is "shattered." Zarathustra, going through all the transformations Empedocles underwent before him, but now "victorious," reacts in a new way to Pana's death. Nietzsche marks the difference with a distancing dash: Zarathustra—laughs. The laugh of the shepherd who has bitten off the head of the snake and spewed it out, the golden laughter that induces Zarathustra's dream of death. "And how I could bear now to die!"

A second "Plan for Zarathustra 4," ramified into twenty-two points, abandons the dramatic form but preserves the melodramatic traits. Some excerpts (*10*, 598–600):

21 [3]†
1. The invitation.
2. The victory procession. The plague-ridden city. The heap of ruins (the old culture burned out).
3. The spring festival with choruses.
4. *Accounting* for themselves before Zarathustra: "What did you do? (did you invent?). . . .
(. . .)
9. Redeem the woman in woman.
(. . .)
21. **Decisive moment**: Zarathustra asks the entire crowd at the festival, "Do you will it all once again?"—everyone replies, "**Yes!**"
With that he dies from happiness.
(the sky cloudless, azure)
(full of premonition, serene, spine-tingling)
(profound stillness, the animals surround Zarathustra, he has veiled his head, has spread his arms over the tablets of stone— appears to be asleep)
the howling dog
something luminous terrifying skims over all their thoughts
The conclusion comprises the speeches of those who swear oaths over his corpse.

The Oath-takers.

22. etc. Magnificent midday as the turning-point—the two paths. The hammer for overwhelming mankind: supreme unfolding of the individual, *so that the individual must begin to perish of himself* (and not, as heretofore, on account of mistakes in his diet!) (*how death came into the world!*)
What happiness!
The creator as self-annihilator! *Creator* out of *goodness* and *wisdom*. All prior morality *outbid*!
At the end, the *swearing of oaths—terrific pledges*!

The howling dog we recognize as the hound that bays in both "On the Vision and the Riddle" and "The Convalescent." It is more hound of hell than tame Dalmatian. The hound howls in such a way that both the vision of time and eternity and the riddle of nausea and nihilism no longer *precede* Zarathustra's convalescence but constitute the very dream of his delirium. Which augurs his death. The "two paths" alluded to in "22. etc." can only be the avenues that meet in the gateway *Augenblick*, "Glance of an Eye." But that would mean that Nietzsche's original manuscript must be restored: the vision and the riddle must be held back from their precocious appearance in Part III of *Thus Spoke Zarathustra* (that is, they must be postponed), in order to be made the backdrop for the oath-takers who stand over Zarathustra's corpse.

One of these oath-takers—whose terrific pledges bind them all to *Untergang*—is Martin Heidegger, inasmuch as what I have just described is no mere fantasy but Heidegger's interpretation of Nietzsche's thought of thoughts during the summer semester of 1937. "Convalescence" is thought confronting ineluctable downgoing.

However, by 1884 Pana has vanished forever, even though we still hear of "the woman who murders" Zarathustra (*11*, 134). Plans continue to demand that he "become hard," that he develop his capacity for annihilation. Some plans emphasize his role as "physician-priest-teacher," after the manner of Empedocles (*11*, 208 and 280–81). Others describe his search for those human beings who "will not perish on account of" the thought of return (*11*, 338). Several plans pause on the verge of Zarathustra's death (*11*, 343), while others plunge into the crater (e.g., *11*, 341†): "the dying Zarathustra holds the earth in an *embrace*.—And although no one had told them, they all knew that Zarathustra was dead."

Here Nietzsche's hero embraces the earth, rather than the corpse of Pana, in death. Nor is Pana present in other later accounts of Zarathustra's demise, from late spring, 1885, after the completion of Part IV. One of these (*11*, 468), a plan for *Midday and Eternity*, shows four "stations," the last entitled "Rise and Fall," *Aufgang und Untergang*. The following directions precede the plan: "He leads his friends ever higher, up to his cave, and finally to the mountaintop: there he dies./—blessing: cavern, Isle of Graves." The preceding plan, marked *nota bene*, reads as follows (*11*, 468†):

> . . . He moved his lips and shut them again; he looked like someone who still had something to say and hesitated to say it. And those who saw him thought they could see a slight blush in his cheek. This lasted a short while: but then, all at once, he shook his head, closed his eyes voluntarily—and died.—
> Thus it transpired that Zarathustra went down.

It remains ambiguous whether Zarathustra dies in the fullness of time, at his acme, affirming and blessing; or in abashed silence and embarrassment, his fundamental teaching not yet having found the words that Zarathustra himself would give it. Or the ears he would elect to hear it. That teaching itself is remarkably ambiguous. In a range of plans drawn up during the autumn months of 1884 through spring of 1885 Nietzsche identifies eternal recurrence as the petrifying head of Medusa.[12] And in these months of explosive poetic creativity Nietzsche composes a large number of lyrics which he hopes to publish as a cycle of *Medusen-Hymnen*. The affinity of eternal recurrence and Medusa emerges from the following fragments (11, 344, 360, 362–64):

29 [31]
> said everything once again (recurring like the **Head of Medusa**

31 [4]
> In Zarathustra 4: the great thought as *Head of Medusa*: all the world's features petrify, a congealed death-throe [*ein gefrorener Todeskampf*].

31 [9]
> Zarathustra 4. (Plan.)
>
> (. . .)
> 6. *The seventh solitude:* —*finally "The Head of Medusa".* (*circa* 40 pages)

Yet the last-mentioned plan exhibits the full ambiguity of eternal recurrence when in its ultimate point, which recounts Zarathustra's final farewell to his mountain cave, it adds the parenthetical remark that here "the consolatory power [*das Tröstliche*] of eternal return shows its face for the first time" (cf. 11, 488). Eternal recurrence: the face of consolation on the Head of Medusa! As duplicitous as Pana herself! As though the name *Medusa* deserved to join those of Ariadne, Corinna, and Pana, claiming a chapter for herself. The last.

Madonna, 1895. Lithograph. Collection, The Museum of Modern Art, New York. The William B. Jaffe and Evelyn A J. Hall Collection.

CHAPTER FOUR

Calina

"So you haven't understood yet?" Rambert shrugged his shoulders almost scornfully.

"Understood what?"

"The plague."

"Ah!" Rieux exclaimed.

"No, you haven't understood that it means exactly that—the same thing over and over and over again."

—Albert Camus, *The Plague*

Climb back down your mountain. It will be cold up there tonight. And if you aren't afraid of being alone in the dark and of the chill in your cave, remember at least that you need other kinds of light and heat than your sun provides. And if you want to meditate on your grand thought tomorrow, come back, sleep a little.

Don't forget the mid-night thought. If tomorrow you want to bring your ultimate depths to the light of day and to hear the voice of your abyss rising in you, come back, plunge into my silence. . . .

—Luce Irigaray, *Amante marine*

At the point he affirms, at the moment he is, loves, the affirmative woman, he [Nietzsche] writes—if one may say such a thing—"with the hand of woman."

—Jacques Derrida, at Cérisy, 1972

MEDUSA'S CHAPTER will have to wait. For we have not yet finished with the *Zarathustra* plans, even though Nietzsche has in the meantime, that is, by April of 1885, brought his great work to a close. The notebooks preserve plans for a Part V, and more sweeping plans as well, as though Nietzsche's book had yet to be begun.

From this cluster of plans, sketched from May through July, 1885, three outlines that will seem quite familiar in some respects, yet in others altogether uncanny (*11*, 541–42):

> 35 [73]†
>
> I. Zarathustra can only *bring good fortune* after the hierarchy has been produced. This must first of all be *taught*.
> II. The hierarchy carried out in a system of world government: ultimately, the Lords of the Earth, a new ruling caste. Springing from them, here and there, an altogether Epicurean god, the overman, who transfigures existence.
> III. Overman's conception of the world. Dionysos.
> IV. Turning back lovingly from this greatest of *alienations* to what is most intimate to him, to the smallest things, Zarathustra *blessing* all his experiences and, as one who blesses, dying.

In this plan, Zarathustra dies for the last time. Dies, as Karl Reinhardt says he must, in order to make room for *Dionysos philosophos*. Is the latter, as a superhuman "conception of the world," precisely that *alienation* from which Zarathustra returns and on account of which he dies? Or may we continue to insist that the Higher Men are alien to Zarathustra, beneath him, so that Zarathustra and Dionysos are recurrences of the same?

Whatever the case, hierarchy, government, legislation, and lordship are by now the central preoccupations of the plans. Which can no longer *afford* to let Zarathustra die and thus become the one he is. For the proposed "Zarathustra 5" (*11*, 541–42), death is reserved for the Christian God, and earth for a race of rulers. The following outline (*11*, 542) introduces the series of images that dominate the plans of the last years:

35 [75]†
1. Zarathustra awakens on the ancient battlement. Hears the heralds' drums.
2. The test: "Do you belong to me?"
3. Procession at the rose-festival.
4. The doctrine of the hierarchy.
5. On the bridge at night. [1]

In August-September of 1885 a more detailed plan incorporates the features we have just seen (*11*, 620):

39 [3]†
Zarathustra 5 (*Youth as the dominant tone*)
   warlike in the highest degree
On an ancient battlement the heralds' drums.
   (Finale) at night, as on the Rialto.
                    the rose-festival.
   Zarathustra the godless hermit, the first solitary who did not pray.
   Are you now strong enough for my truths?
   Who belongs to me? what is noble?
"*Are you such?*" (as refrain) the hierarchy: and you would have to have everything in you in order to be able to rule, but also *beneath* you!

   Refrain: and if you cannot say, "We revere them, yet we are of a higher kind," then you are not of *my* kind.

   The rose-festival.
   On the bridge at night.

The plan goes on to elaborate the notions of hierarchy and dominion, garlanded by the imagery of medieval pageantry and girded by the nascent structures of "*The Will to Power*: Attempt at a New Interpretation of All Occurrence" (*11*, 619; cf. 629, 661). Zarathustra's city is now far from Motley Cow, and even more remote from Acragas. Certainly no womancity.

"Zarathustra pacing the walls of the battlement:—he hears absolute pessimism being preached. The city is surrounded. He is silent" (*11*, 628†).

The next cluster of *Zarathustra* plans, from the autumn of 1885 through spring, 1886 (*12*, 47–48; cf. 61), reintroduces woman in the figure of Ariadne proper. But in eerie guise.

1 [162]†

The orgiastic soul.—
I have seen him [*ihn*]: his eyes, at least—sometimes profoundly calm, sometimes green and slippery honey-eyes
his halcyon smile,
the sky looked on, bloody and cruel

the orgiastic soul of woman
I have seen him [*ihn*], his halcyon smile, his honey-eyes, sometimes deep and veiled, sometimes green and slippery, a trembling superficies,

slippery, sleepy, trembling, hesitating,
heaves the sea that is his eyes

1 [163]†
1. Caesar among pirates
2. On the bridge
3. The wedding. —and suddenly, as the sky grows dark
4. Ariadne.

1 [164]†
This music—isn't it Dionysian?
the dance?
the cheerfulness? the tempter?
the religious flood?
under Plato's pillow Ar[istophanes]?

1 [165]†
our vagabond musicians and human beings of dishonorable burial—they are the nearest kin to witches, they have their haunted hills

1 [166]†
mystic nature, besmirched with vices and raging

1 [167]†
the generous, pristine font that could never come to terms with the single drop of filth that dropped into it, until finally it turned ochreous, noxious through and through: the corrupted angels

Green eyes of the voluptuous soul, iridescent with the emerald beauty of Dionysos. Dionysos among pirates, on his way to Ariadne on Naxos. The nuptials of Dionysos and Ariadne, the hymeneal "halcyon songs" that Nietzsche plans to write as a "recuperation" from the labors of *Thus Spoke Zarathustra* (see *12*, 61 and 68). Yet the notes headed "The orgiastic soul" and "the orgiastic soul of woman" can be read in at least two very different ways. First, the fragments themselves may actually speak *as* the soul, so that the words "I have seen him" refer to the god as their object; the fragments themselves ought to stand in quotation marks, inasmuch as what we have here is an addendum to Ariadne's lament. Second, the word *him* might be taken as referring to the soul itself, so that the titles would be, not indicators of the narrative voice, but the object under discussion. The first reading would require that we reopen the question as to why and how Nietzsche intends to speak (or write) through the orgiastic soul of woman. Difficult and dangerous enough. Yet the second would require even more astonishing upsets.

What could we possibly make of a radical inversion—rather, subversion—of genders, such that the soul (*die Seele*, feminine) is addressed as "him," even when it is the orgiastic, oriental soul of woman? Such inversion occurs in a far less conspicuous way in the episode of *Thus Spoke Zarathustra*, Part I, "On Chastity" (4, 69–70; cf. *10*, 24–25):

> I love the forest. It is a poor thing to live in cities: there are too many in heat [*brünstig*] there.
> Is it not better to fall into the hands of a murderer than into the dreams of a woman in heat?
> Just look at these men, I ask you: their eyes say it—they know of nothing better on earth than lying with a woman.
> Mire covers the bottoms of their souls; and woe if that mire still has spirit!

The dream of the woman in heat is dreamt behind the eyes of the male; her moist ground is the muck of his soul. Nietzsche's focus here is on the male, the man infected by woman: "These people do restrain themselves: but the bitch sensuality leers enviously out of everything they do. . . ." Nietzsche is following an old tradition—although in what way these things are "given over" as a tradition is an arresting question, one that would alter our traditional use of the word *traditio*—that attributes sensuality as such, ἀφροδίσια ἀκολασία, to the female. To the female that looks out of a man's eyes after she has ravaged his soul.[2]

In a note sketched during the year 1884 Nietzsche writes (*11*, 192):

> Women are far more sensuous than men (although their ingrained pudicity makes a secret of it even to them): for males, there are ultimately more impor-

tant functions than the sexual. But when a handsome man comes near a woman—women are altogether unable to contemplate a relationship between man and woman that would not entail a sexual tension.

Again the distancing dash separates the writer's hand from both "woman" and "women." Yet Nietzsche knows that without the soil at the bottom of his soul nothing in him that is writer or thinker can flourish. He knows that without the exchange and ringdance of male/female in him he cannot create. Hence the "doubling" of sex that appears so often in his poetry and thought. Perhaps we ought to pause to examine several examples of this, not the most obvious ones, not the examples most often discussed in the literature.

The experience of "Sils-Maria," both as place and poem (3, 649), is essentially one of reduplication—when "one became two," and Zarathustra was suddenly there in full poetic power. Nietzsche's "Aftersong" to *Beyond Good and Evil*, "From High Mountains" (5, 241–43), also emphasizes a doubling and a movement toward alterity. When the singer's friends return to Sils in order to visit the poet after a long separation, they are discomfited by what they find:

> I—am no longer the one you seek?
>   Have hand, footfall, face been exchanged?
> And *what* I am, to you friends—am I not that?
>
> Did I become another? And foreign to myself?
>   Sprung from myself?[3]

The poem's concluding verses, added in the spring of 1886, invoke the poet-charlatan-wizard of *Thus Spoke Zarathustra*, Part IV, and the doubling at Sils-Maria that spawned Zarathustra:

> The midday friend! No, don't ask who—
> At midday one turned into two. . . .

Friend Zarathustra is "the guest of guests" at the "wedding of light and dark." The festivities last long: Giorgio Colli reports (5, 421) that the only lines of his oeuvres that Nietzsche ever tried to recollect during the years of his insanity were lines of "From High Mountains."

The doubling of the sex of the narrative voice, or the blurring of the lines between such sexes, occurs throughout Nietzsche's work. In "Little Women, Old and Young" (ASZ I; 4, 84-86) it is not entirely clear what Zarathustra is "so anxious to protect" beneath his "cloak." The only thing that is clear about this episode—the most notorious of Nietzsche's misogynist texts—is that the whip Zarathustra carries to women never leaves the hand of Lou.[4]

We have already witnessed the bizarre duplicity of Sorcerer and Ariadne, a duplicity to which "the orgiastic soul of woman" would return us. Yet the remaining lyrics of *Thus Spoke Zarathustra*, Part IV, all of them destined to become *Dionysos Dithyrambs*, betray the same exigency. The doddering magician's *second* song, "The Song of Melancholy," destined to become the dithyramb "Only Fool! Only Poet!", is introduced in the following way (4, 370-71):

> "Just open your eyes! He [the spirit of melancholy] loves to come *naked*; whether he's male or female I can't tell yet, but he's coming, compelling me; O woe, open all your senses!
> "The day subsides, evening bends over all things now, even the best things; look now, and listen, you Higher Men, what sort of devil, whether man or woman, this spirit of eventide-melancholy is!"

Finally, the most astonishing doubling occurs in the song of Nietzsche's own (or Zarathustra's own) "Wanderer and Shadow," the song entitled "Among Daughters of the Desert" (4, 379–85). From its extravagant parody of German (and European) exotica from Luther to Goethe let me cite only a few lines.

> Here now I sit
> In this tiniest of oases,
> Like a date,
> Brown and O so sweet, oozing gold, lecherous
> For the round mouth of a maid,
> Or better still a young girl's
> Ice-cold snow-white cutting
> Incisors: after these the heart
> Of all hot dates hankers. Selah.

Zarathustra's shadow goes on to picture himself surrounded by two exotic "maiden cats," intimate Dudù and, fresh from the West-East Divan, sultry Suleika; not merely surrounded but "transphinxed" by them: *umsphinxt*. That word is crammed full of meanings, the singer warns us, begging God's forgiveness for his "linguistic sin." The neighboring datepalms he pictures as the fluttering skirts of dancing girls—girls who have "lost a leg":

> She's lost it!
> It's gone!
> Gone to eternity!
> The other leg!
> O what a shame, that lovely other leg!
> Where might it be tarrying, weeping forlorn?

The lonely leg?
Perhaps affrighted by a
Voracious yellowish flaxenhaired
Beastie of a lion? Or by now
Crunched and munched away—
O mercy, woe is me, munched away! Selah.

The shadow now tries to cheer the maiden cats that surround and transphinx
him. He urges them not to cry, in fitting words:

Weep no more,
Pallid Dudu!
Be a man, Suleika!

No comment. Except to say that *umsphinxt* means (if more linguistic sins are
possible) not merely *surrounded by* sphinxes but *transformed into* a sphinx, *en-
sphinxed*, as it were, become the "young woman's body" that "seduces us to
existence."[5] Zarathustra's shadow wanders fairly far.

But enough. It is time to restore order to my own text, which is getting
out of hand. Losing whatever leg it has to stand on. Evading the issues. For
the hilarity, histrionics, and hysteria ought not to be allowed to conceal the
astonishing ambivalence of Nietzsche's sensuality, its doublings and folds, its
blurrings and confusions. This same hilarious Nietzsche can praise the Stoa
for its aloofness "in the midst of Hellenistic civilization, in an atmosphere
suffused with Aphrodisiac fragrances and gone lecherous" (5, 110); can be-
moan the lewdness of the Higher Men, who subserve their "inner beasts,"
cater to their "swine" (4, 362-63; cf. 377); can extol "the victor, the self-
compeller, the commander of the senses, the master of his virtues . . . ,
square-shouldered in body and soul" (4, 90). Yet he can at the same time and
almost in the same breath be the unerring anatomist of "moral castratism"
and flight from the body. We dare not forget the keen analyses in *Twilight of
the Idols* (6, 74; 82-83) in which even the epistemologist's denigration of the
senses is traced back to the flight from sensuality; or those unsurpassed pages
of *Toward a Genealogy of Morals*, Part III, "What Are Ascetic Ideals?" (5,
339–412), which reveal the extraordinary depth of Nietzsche's genealogy of
the genealogist. Himself.

I shall restore order by turning now to the very last plans for Nietzsche's
Zarathustran drama. Let us examine three of these plans quite closely. First,
a detailed plan from the years 1885–86, perhaps the last such plan Nietzsche
sketched. It summarizes much of what we have seen already, yet omits several
crucial aspects and personages of the earlier plans (*12*, 128-29):

2 [129]†

The Eternal Return.
Zarathustran Dances and Processions.
First Part: God's Wake.
by
Friedrich Nietzsche.

1. God's Wake.
2. At magnificent midday.
3. "Where is the hand for this hammer?"
4. We oath-takers.

I.

The plague-ridden city. He is warned; he is not afraid, and enters the city, veiled. All sorts of pessimism pass in review. The soothsayer *interprets* every element in the procession. The addiction to Other, the addiction to No, and finally the addiction to Nothing follow one another.

At length Zarathustra provides the *explanation*: God is dead, this is the *cause* of the gravest danger: but why? it could also be cause for the grandest encouragement!

II.

The arrival of his friends.

Enjoyment, among the ones who go down, of *the one who is perfect*: those in withdrawal.

The friends give an accounting.

Festive parades. The decisive time, magnificent midday.

The great thanksgiving and requiem-offering to the dead God.

III.

The new task.	The death of God, for
Means for the task.	the soothsayer the most
His friends abandon	terrifying event, is the
him.	most fortunate and propitious for Zarathustra.

Zarathustra dies.

IV. We Oath-takers

The centrality of Zarathustra's death in the third act is made evident by its position on the page. It may be intimated already in Act II by the striking phrase, "Enjoyment, among the ones who go down [*der Untergehenden*], of *the one who is perfect* [*an* dem Vollkommenen]: those in withdrawal [*Abzieh-ende*]." The grounds for Zarathustra's demise appear to be bifurcated into the two columns of Act III. We are familiar by now with the grief Zarathustra experiences when his disciples forsake him. Yet what is the precise relationship between the death of God, as a propitious event, and Zarathustra's own death? On the one hand, joy and encouragement, the open seas espied in *The Gay Science* and in several poems; on the other hand, the turmoil among Zarathustra's friends (the Higher Men), who are unprepared for the thought of eternal return. Only in the fourth act, over Zarathustra's dead body, will the oath of unstinting affirmation be sworn.

One further postponement, the last, involving the remaining two plans (*12*, 93–94). Among these "friends" who abandon Zarathustra and so occasion his death, where is Pana? Or Corinna? Ariadne? Or has the name changed again?

2 [71] †
For "Zarathustra."

Calina: brown-red, everything too acrid nearby. Highest sun. Ghostlike.

Sipo Matador.

And who says this is not what we want? What music and seduction! Nothing there that would not poison, allure, gnaw, overthrow, transvalue

I The *decisive* moment:

The hierarchy. 1) Shatter the good and the just!
                             2)

The eternal return.

Midday and Eternity.
The Soothsayer's Book.

2 [72] †

Midday and Eternity.
by
F. N.

I The Wake. Zarathustra finds himself at a great festival:
II The New Hierarchy.
III On the Lords of the Earth.
IV On the Ring of Return.

Here we witness the transition from the project of "Zarathustra" to that of "Midday and Eternity," the latter devoted to hierarchy and lordship. The thought of eternal recurrence remains the apotheosis. Yet it is no longer entangled in the story of (the) woman; it is no longer the burden of downgoing and mortality. It is a doctrine for the lords of the earth. And the earth herself? Who, or what, is this "Calina"? Calina, "for 'Zarathustra.' " Is she the third woman, the third casket, of leaden love?

Her identity is clear—if it is a she—inasmuch as the words "Shatter the good and the just!" appear in an earlier plan (25 [453] 1884; *11*, 134) as the very words of the "pious" woman who murders Zarathustra. Auburn-haired Calina would then complement the ugliest man, who murders God out of shame. Yet how would the pious woman elicit such epithets of forbidden pleasure, of the risk of death ("And who says this is not what we want?"), gnawing poison (as of a plague), irresistible allurement, music and seduction? The words immediately above these in the plan read: "Sipo Matador." A reference to the romance of far-off Spain? Ogygia? A number of poetic fragments suggest it (see, for example, *11*, 332 and 621). But no: a passage in *Beyond Good and Evil* (5, 207) identifies "Sipo Matador" as a Javanese plant, a parasitical vine that winds about the sturdiest trees, clambering to their crowns and killing them. "Calina" might refer to *salina*, salt pits, which would account for the pungency; or to alkaline earth, the caustic base that Hegel identified as the specifically womanly power of universal, elemental nature, *Kali*; or to the *saline* solution of the blood, which would explain the color. And the danger. Yet whoever or whatever Calina may be, why is the sun at its zenith? It is midday, to be sure, the hour of eternal recurrence; but what binds Calina (or any woman) to noontide and to Nietzsche's thought of thoughts? Finally, and most enigmatically, how can the sun at its apogee be "ghostlike," *gespenstisch*? As though midday and midnight were the same. As though Calina's were the ghostly beauty of the sailing ship, the dream and the risk of death.

Calina is cited twice in lists of poems from the autumn of 1884, the time of "The Travail of the Woman in Childbirth" (*11*, 312–13[†]). The second of these lists bears the title "Midday Thoughts." *Calina* is number 24 in the first list, number 11 in the second:

(. . .)
24 *Calina* brown-red, everything too acrid nearby
   in high summer. Ghostly (my *current* danger!)

(. . .)
11 Calina: my current danger, in high summer, ghostly, brown-red, everything
   too acrid nearby

Somewhere someone sees clearly and distinctly—with Maenadic sharpsightedness—who or what Calina is. He or she at this moment is writing about her or it. Checking the *Diccionario de la lengua española* of the Royal Academy in Madrid, noting that Calina (from the Latin *caligo, caliginis*, "mark upon the brow," or "darkness and obscurity") is a feminine noun referring to an atmospheric disturbance caused by either water vapor or dust that pollutes the air, wondering whether Calina is the *Fata morgana* transferred from the Straits of Messina to the Castilian Meseta. By way of Java. "For 'Zarathustra.'" Obscurely. We ourselves will be patient, trusting in science. We will not mislay our umbrella, will not lose our leg.

If this chapter began as a circumvention of Medusa, let it remain that to the end. We shall abandon Calina now for Ariadne, reverting to the central figure of the very last plans and sketches. Where we began.

A long plan from autumn, 1887 (*12*, 400–02[†]), proffers "for consideration" a project Nietzsche calls "the *perfect book.*" Certain traits of this perfect book remind us of the drama plans from 1870 through 1886. The perfect book is a "monologue of ideas," and is innocent of scholarly trappings or argumentative demonstrations; it is "absolutely *personal*," yet there is "no ego in it"; it is like a conversation of "spirits," even though the most abstract things present themselves in "flesh and blood" on its pages; its words are explicit, even "military" in their commanding simplicity, although the perfect book describes the states of the "most intellectual" human beings. Most intriguing is the notion that the book is to be constructed along the lines of a tragedy, "aiming toward a *catastrophe.*" Other plans (*12*, 100; cf. *5*, 409) cite the necessity of such catastrophe, one of them as follows (*12*, 395):

(. . .)
6) slow, deceptive, Labyrinth
7) **Minotaur**, *catastrophe* (the thought to which one must offer human sacrifice—the more, the better!)

And following the catastrophe, succeeding upon it, as at an Athenian festival:

Satyr-play
at the Conclusion

Blend in: brief conversations among Theseus, Dionysos, and Ariadne.

"Theseus is becoming absurd," said Ariadne. "Theseus is becoming virtuous." Theseus jealous because of Ariadne's dream.[6] The hero marveling at himself, becoming absurd.

Plaint of Ariadne
Dionysos devoid of jealousy: "The thing I love about you—how could a
Theseus love that?" . . .
Last Act. Marriage of Dionysos and Ariadne
"One is not jealous when one is god," said Dionysos, "unless it be of gods."

> "Ariadne," said Dionysos, "you are a labyrinth: Theseus got lost in you, he
> no longer holds the thread; what good does it do him now that the Minotaur did
> not devour him? The thing that is eating away at him is worse than a Minotaur."
> "You flatter me," replied Ariadne. "But I weary of my pity; all heroes should
> perish on account of me. That is my ultimate love for Theseus: 'I shall see to it
> that he perishes' "

These notes allow us to see why the final lines of Nietzsche's "Plaint of
Ariadne" have such a jarring effect and seem so out of place. They are in
fact lines from a satyr-play. They are essentially "displaced" from the tragedy.
Ariadne's own words here have lost their tragic pathos as well: while Theseus
is becoming absurd, Ariadne grows sardonic. When the tragic hero moons
over her, she refuses compassion: "I shall see to it that he perishes." Yet even
here the Labyrinth pertains to her, and not even Dionysos can dispossess her
of it. Another fragment from the same period (12, 510) reads:

> "Oh, Ariadne, you yourself are the Labyrinth: one doesn't ever get out of you
> again". . . .
> "Dionysos, you flatter me: you are divine". . . .

Nietzsche had been trying his hand at such satyr-play for some time. Indeed, it constituted an essential part of his strategy from 1885 on. In
Beyond Good and Evil (5, 42–43) he called for a free-spirited philosophy that
would always and everywhere be satyr-play: the philosophy of the future was
not to be a pious martyrdom for the sake of a Truth from which the saving
grace of humor had been drained, leaving only a noxious sediment of vengeance and asceticism. Nietzsche knew full well that to define philosophy from
the satyr's point of view would be to transform it from tragedy to farce. The
philosophy of the future, beyond good and evil—"merely a satyr-play, a farc-
ical postlude, an extended proof of the fact that the long tragedy proper *has
come to an end*: presupposing that every philosophy, in its genesis, was a protracted tragedy."

Consider, as an illustration, the astonishing note on "Morality and
Physiology," from the summer of 1885 (11, 576–79). The note expounds ear-
nestly and at length the complexities of the human body, when suddenly one
of those double-dashes appears——and then the following:

> Talking a mile a minute this way, I gave my didactic drive free reign, for I was
> delighted to have somebody there who could stand to listen to me. Yet at pre-

cisely this point Ariadne couldn't take it any longer—the whole affair took place during my first sojourn on Naxos—and she said, "But my dear sir, you speak a swinish sort of German!" —"It's German," I replied cheerfully, "just plain old German. Leave the swine out of it, my dear goddess! You underestimate the difficulty of saying fine things in German!" — "Fine things!" cried Ariadne, horrified. "But that was sheer positivism! Proboscis philosophy! A mish-mash, a farmer's load of concepts from a hundred different philosophies! Where on earth are you going with all that?" —As she said this she toyed impatiently with that famous thread, the one that once guided her Theseus through the Labyrinth. —In this way it came to light that Ariadne's philosophical education was about two millennia behind the times.

Karl Reinhardt notes (331), with some justice, that this risible anecdote, like virtually all the others of Nietzsche's final years, is worthy of the *Journal des Goncourts*; he observes also that if Ariadne's philosophical education is in arrears it is only because Nietzsche is trying to revivify a myth that comes two millennia too late. In these repartees between Dionysos and Ariadne, Nietzsche is aiming at a particular kind of inanity (*adventavit asinus*), the high hilarity of "The Ass Festival" in *Thus Spoke Zarathustra*, Part IV. Aiming, but missing.

A second specimen. In a note from spring or summer of 1888 (*13*, 498) that was taken up into *Twilight of the Idols* (*6*, 123–24), Nietzsche discusses the anthropomorphic character of aesthetic judgments. A higher judge of taste, he says, might overthrow all our most confident aesthetic judgments and principles. The text then shifts dramatically to the following dialogue, without the double-dash, but with ellipsis points. . . .

> "Oh, Dionysos, divine one, why are you pulling my ears?" Ariadne once asked during one of those famous conversations on Naxos with her philosophical lover. "I find a kind of humor in your ears, Ariadne: why aren't they even longer?"

Warum sind sie nicht noch länger? The implication is that Ariadne already has donkey ears, that she is the *Eselin* who is always on thin ice. [7]

In September and October of 1888, the months of intense activity that produced *The Wagner Case*, *The Antichrist*, *Twilight of the Idols*, and *Ecce Homo*, we find the very last plans and titles that invoke the name "Zarathustra." "Zarathustra's Temptation" and "Zarathustra's Songs" are juxtaposed (see *13*, 589–90). The latter are soon to be called *Dionysos Dithyrambs*. Among the scattered, disjointed fragments of verse that we find from the summer of 1888 there are two that expose the fate of an Empedoclean thinking that feels so compelled to legislate that little is left for song (*13*, 570):

20 [127] [†]
a thought,

still liquid hot, lava:
yet all lava builds
about itself a fortress,
every thought crushes
itself at last with "laws"

20 [128][†]
when no new voice arose to speak
you made of the old words
a law:
when life congeals, law looms large

In the towering law, in the clinkers of legislative, valuative thought, a disarming violence. More than *disarming*.

In the famous Preface to *Beyond Good and Evil* ("Presupposing that truth is a woman—") Nietzsche ridicules the dogmatic philosopher who tries to force revelations and seize truths. And in "The Flies of the Marketplace" Zarathustra enjoins, "Do not be jealous of things that are compelling and unconditional, O lover of truth! Never yet did truth cling to the arm of something unconditional."

Among the verses for "Zarathustra's Songs," the following lines late in 1888 (*13*, 557–58), lines of weariness, desperation, and postponement beyond recovery:

20 [48][†]
Truth—
a woman, nothing better:
guileful in her shame:
what she most wants
she refuses to know,
raises a warning finger. . . .
To whom will she yield? To force alone!
—So use force,
be hard, you who are most wise!
you must compel her,
the abashed truth . . .
for her felicity
compulsion is needed—
—she is a woman, nothing better. . . .

"Force alone!" appears to bring me full-circle to my initial doubts and suspicions, my initial desire to disengage Nietzsche's identification of truth and woman from the banalities and analities of misogyny. Yet the acrid obscurity of Calina frustrates such disengagement, as it deflects and defuses all "Force alone!"

But is it necessary—or even possible—to confront these postponements I claim to have espied in Nietzsche's thinking and writing? What would such confrontation be like? Is it not otiose to force the face-to-face of confrontation onto the back-to-back of postponement?

Let me review the curious ideas and images limned in this book and try to make a case for them. If no law. Let me try—because I do not want Nietzsche's destiny as my own. Would prefer to lose him. Yet only the hand of woman, the writing hand, the hand back to which the trace of thread always leads us, can loosen the grip of that destiny. Gingerly.

Derrida believes that Nietzsche possesses such a hand. So do I. Must it wither?

I began with the ambiguity of apotropaic sails and spurring spars, advancing to the theme of *distance*, the evanescence of pure presence, the embarcation of every in-itself on a journey with no destination. For Nietzsche himself, as "We Artficers!" betrays, the action at a distance of woman itself calls for distance, if not flight: the naturalness of the sensuous, sensual body, the body (of) woman, fundamentally concealing and deceiving, radiant and dissembling at once, evokes the terror that comes to a head in Medusa. Yet a genealogy of the pathos of distance would presumably show that distance from the sensuous body is essentially Christian-ascetic and not at all Greek.

My question therefore became: In what way do woman, sensuality, and death form a single constellation in Nietzsche's thought; and why does Nietzsche's thinking postpone confrontation with that triad? In order to prevent Nietzsche's postponements from becoming my own commonplaces, these four chapters tried to discern the postponements as they *take place* in Nietzsche's work, especially in the notebooks. I began a second time, taking up Karl Reinhardt's analysis of Ariadne's lament. Reinhardt's thesis, pushed to its extreme, is that Nietzsche's later philosophy tries to become woman. Tries to reach Dionysos by exposing itself without reserve to all the agonies and vulnerabilities of Ariadne. However much the complement Dionysos-Ariadne may degenerate into burlesque, satyr-play, and farce, the seriousness and risk of Nietzsche's venture cannot be doubted.

That venture begins with a search for the mothers of tragedy. At first Dionysos does not make a very good mother, inasmuch as his domestication deprives her of all his accoutrements. At least until Nietzsche contemplates the orgiastic soul of woman—and all his traits. Even then the question of how one can *show* Dionysos, reveal what is essentially concealed *as* concealed, remains baffling. The fate of Oedipus, the last philosopher, the last human being, the last voice, having transgressed against all the limits, dispels our expectations concerning any straightforward revelation of Dionysos. He or she is the abyss of sensuality on whose verge philosophy experiences vertigo. Not in Kant first of all, nor even in Plato, but in Empedocles. The tragic philosopher. *Actio in distans*, love and hate, the unity of myth, art, and science in the physician of culture: Empedocles. Not to be included in a treatise on philosophy in the tragic age of the Greeks but to act out the tragedy as such, to be put on stage, or, at least, be portrayed on the theatrical page. In order to perform, if not as an over-hero, then as a kind of under-hero.

Perform how? Do what? Fall in love, with a woman. A beauty. An infestation. Woman as nature and the sufferings of the world, Schopenhauerian will, will o' the wisp, and woe. Whose love is a curse, a plague, an access of pity and fear, up to the final fiery purge. And so Empedocles is made to take the plunge. Not alone. With woman. Made to fall . . . in love. To restore the heat that remained around the middle of her body. To play at being Dionysos. To act a part, ridiculously infatuated with Corinna, and then to run. Dionysos fleeing in the face of Ariadne, skirting her like the plague. Corinna-Ariadne, the mortal woman in whom the announcement of rebirth unleashes an ecstasy of death.

Ten years later in Nietzsche's life comes the announcement proper: the thought of eternal recurrence of the same. It comes in the reduplicated figure of Zarathustra, who goes down to humankind in order to teach overman. Who postpones the consequences of his own teaching, invents a consolation for himself, flirts with eternity, skirting the gateway of time and the dance of life like the plague. Who follows the footprints of Empedocles up to the crater's rim. But not into it. Unless to fetch the devil.

Meanwhile, in the notebooks, Nietzsche is plotting Zarathustra's demise. Zarathustra will die as a result of the pain inflicted when his followers recoil from eternal return, a teaching that is always premature; of his own task, whereby the mildest must become hardest, and all rigor go to *rigor mortis*; of the vision of eternal return itself, and the joy that Zarathustra cannot sustain, inasmuch as he himself is not overman; of contact with a woman in the plague-ridden city, a woman Zarathustra heals. Radically. Or Zarathustra will die of snake bite, from his own discernment. Or, having embraced the cadaver of the woman he has cured and killed, he will choke (as the Greeks said) on bread baked in cold ovens. His own golden sarcophagus will then plunge into fiery Etna.

Or he will die of knife wounds, self-inflicted, or proffered by Pana. Pana-Ariadne. Will die of pity for her pity. Because of the suffering his felicity has caused her, or the pangs of his own contempt. Will die because "We killed him." Will die when his happiness and fortune stand in horrific contrast, when his way up is his way down. Will die, until, finally, in the plans for Part IV, the grounds for his dying at all will have become hopelessly obscure: Pana wants to kill him; she lies there, shattered; he laughs, ascends the face of the mountain, dies his happy death. Embracing the earth, but no longer Pana. Dies his happy death, rapt to the face of consolation. On the head of Medusa.

Calina, burnt sienna, pungent earth or vapor at high noon: an exotic of midday and eternity. A ghost. Nowhere to be seen at the festival of roses, amid the pomp and circumstance of legislation, on the hobby-horse of re-valuation. Nor at God's wake. Calina tarrying in the vicinity of Ariadne, somewhere between Java and the Straits of Messina, between defiled and salubrious water, histrionics and seductive music, desert and jungle, bloody and azure skies. Calina-Ariadne. On the emerald green sea. Slippery, sleepy, trembling superficies. Heaves the sea that is his eyes. His. The orgiastic soul of woman behind the eyes of poet and thinker, thinker and poet of the doubling. *Umsphinxt.*

Why does Nietzsche (not to lose him just yet, lest the question recoil) never write the perfect book? Why does he sketch only a scene or two of the satyr-play that is to cap it, the tragedy and its catastrophe postponed from beginning to end? After scores of plans, projections, and sketches? One may certainly look for plausible explanations in the realm of what we call Nietzsche's "life."[8] Seeking Ariadne where there was only Cosima, Corinna where there was only Trampedach, Pana where there was only Lou. Not to forget the mother of the tragedy—who when Nietzsche was pronounced incurably harmless and released from the asylum enthused to Overbeck, "Again and again my soul is filled with gratitude to our dear, good God, that I can now *take care of* this child of my heart. . . ."

Yet may one also look elsewhere? To the ineluctable necessity of displacement, doubling, and blurring of the lines in Nietzsche's own writing? To satyr-play as *postponement* of the tragedy, but a postponement that is *in pursuit*, relentlessly? Theseus chasing the Ariadnic thread. The under-hero, and not the god, unless as Zagreus: Dionysos in pieces. Who loses the thread, never gets out, is lost. Or who is ultimately more dedicated to groping his way through the labyrinth than to escaping or fleeing in the face of it. No matter what is eating away at him. Or who.

Corinna, Pana, Calina. All the pleats and plaints of Ariadne. Not to be skirted. All the duplicities.

APPENDIX: The Principal German Texts

This Appendix gives the German texts of quotations marked with a dagger (†). I have selected those passages from Nietzsche's notebooks that are least accessible to the general reader yet which are important to my own reading. I excluded texts Nietzsche himself published, trusting that readers will have access to these through any of a number of German editions. An occasional note comments on peculiarities in the text or difficulties in the translation. The page numbers in the left-hand margin refer to the page in this book where the quotation begins; the number above each passage is the Mette-number, with year, and the volume and page of the *Kritische Studienausgabe*.

Page	*German Texts*

19   28 [9] 1884; *11*, 302
Ich liege still —
ausgestreckt,
Halbtodtem gleich, dem man die Füsse wärmt
—die Käfer fürchten sich vor mir[1]

45   5 [116] 1870–71; *7*, 125
Act I. E⟨mpedokles⟩ stürzt den Pan, der ihm die Antwort verweigert. Er fühlt sich geächtet.
Die Agrigentiner wollen ihn zum König wählen, unerhörte Ehren. Er erkennt den Wahn der Religion, nach langem Kampfe.
Die Krone wird ihm von der schönsten Frau dargebracht.
II. Furchtbare Pest, er bereitet große Schauspiele, dionysische Bacchanale, die Kunst offenbart sich als Prophetin des Menschenwehs. Das Weib als die Natur.
III. Er beschließt bei einer Leichenfeier das Volk zu vernichten, um es von der Qual zu befrein. Die Überlebenden der Pest sind ihm noch bemitleidenswerther.
Bei dem Pantempel. „Der große Pan ist todt."

46   5 [117] 1870–71; 7, 125

Das Weib in der Theatervorstellung, stürzt heraus und sieht den Geliebten niedersinken. Sie will zu ihm, Empedokles hält sie zurück und entdeckt seine Liebe zu ihr. Sie giebt nach, der Sterbende spricht, Empedokles entsetzt sich vor der ihm offenbarten Natur.

46   5 [118] 1870–71; 7, 126

Empedocles, der durch alle Stufen, Religion Kunst Wissenschaft getrieben wird und die letzte auflösend gegen sich selbst richtet.[2]

Aus der Religion durch die Erkenntniß daß sie Trug ist.

Jetzt Lust am künstlerischen Scheine, daraus durch das erkannte Weltleiden getrieben. Das Weib als die Natur.

Jetzt betrachtet er als Anatom das Weltleiden, wird Tyrann, der Religion und Kunst benutzt, und verhärtet sich immer mehr. Er beschließt Vernichtung des Volks, weil er dessen Unheilbarkeit erkannt hat. Das Volk, um den Krater versammelt: er wird wahnsinnig und verkündet vor seinem Verschwinden die Wahrheit der Wiedergeburt. Ein Freund stirbt mit ihm.[3]

47   8 [30] 1870–72; 7, 233–34[4]

Griechisches Erinnerungsfest. Zeichen des Verfalls. Ausbruch der Pest. Der Homerrhapsode. Empedokles erscheint als Gott, um zu heilen.

Die Ansteckung durch Furcht und Mitleid. Gegenmittel die Tragödie. Als eine Nebenperson stirbt, will die Heldin zu ihm. Empedokles hält sie entflammt zurück, sie erglüht für ihn. Empedokles schaudert vor der Natur.

Ausbreitung der Pest.

Letzter Festtag—Opfer des Pan am Aetna. Empedokles prüft Pan und zertrümmert ihn. Das Volk flüchtet. Die Heldin bleibt. Empedokles im Übermaß des Mitleids will sterben. Er geht in den Schlund und ruft noch „Fliehe!"—Sie: Empedokles! und folgt ihm. Ein Thier rettet sich zu ihnen. Lava um sie herum.

47   8 [31]

Aus einem apollinischen Gott wird ein todessüchtiger Mensch.

Aus der Stärke seiner pessimistischen Erkenntniß wird er böse.

Im hervorbrechenden Übermaß des Mitleides erträgt er das Dasein nicht mehr.

Er kann die Stadt nicht heilen, weil sie von der griechischen Art abgefallen ist.

Er will sie radikal heilen, nämlich vernichten, hier aber rettet sie ihre griechische Art.

In seiner Göttlichkeit will er helfen.

Als mitleidiger Mensch will er vernichten.

Als Dämon vernichtet er sich selbst.

Immer leidenschaftlicher wird Empedokles.

48   8 [37]

I. Morgengrauen. ⟨I.⟩ Pausanias trägt einen Kranz zu Corinna. Der Wächter erzählt seine Erscheinungen (Aetna). 2. Eine Gruppe Landleute kommen: das über Empedokles phantasierende Mädchen, plötzlich todt. 3. Corinna sieht den entsetzten Pausanias. Besänftigungsscene. Sie wiederholen ihre Rollen: bei dem Hauptsatze schweigt Pausanias finster und kann sich nicht erinnern. 4. Ein klagender Aufzug, lyrisch. 5. Volksscene, die Furcht vor der Pest. 6. Der Rhapsode. 7. Empedokles, mit Opferpfannen, Pausanias in Entsetzen vor seinen Füßen. Es wird ganz hell. Corinna gegen Empedocles.[5]

II. Im Rath. Empedokles verhüllt vor einem Altar. Die Rathsherrn kommen einzeln, heiter und jedesmal über den Verhüllten erschreckt. „Die Pest ist unter euch! Seid Griechen!" Furcht und Mitleid verboten. Lächerliche Rathsscene. Aufregung des Volks. Der Saal wird gestürmt. Die Königskrone angeboten. Empedokles ordnet die Tragödie an und vertröstet auf den Aetna, wird verehrt. Vorstellung der Tragödie: Corinna's Schauder.

III. Der Chor.
Pausanias und Corinna. Theseus und Ariadne.
Empedokles und Corinna auf der Bühne.
Todestaumel des Volks bei der Verkündigung der Wiedergeburt. Er wird als Gott Dionysus verehrt, während er wieder anfängt mitzuleiden. Der Schauspieler Dionysus

lächerlich in Corinna verliebt.

Die zwei Mörder, die die Leiche fortschaffen.

Böse Vernichtungslust des Empedocles räthselhaft kund-
gegeben.

IV. Proclamation des Empedocles über das Abendfest. Taumel
des Volks, das sicher durch das Erscheinen des Gottes ist.
Greise Mutter und Korinna. Höchste Beruhigung.
Im Haus der Corinna. Empedokles kommt finster zurück.

V. Empedokles unter den Schülern.
Nachtfeier.
Mystische Mitleidsrede. Vernichtung des Daseinstriebs,
Tod des Pan.
Flucht des Volks.
Zwei Lavaströme, sie können nicht entrinnen!
Empedokles und Corinna. Empedokles fühlt sich als Mör-
der, unendlicher Strafe werth, er hofft eine Wiedergeburt
des Sühnetodes. Dies treibt ihn in den Aetna. Er will Kor-
inna retten. Ein Thier kommt zu ihnen. Korinna stirbt mit
ihm. „Flieht Dionysus vor Ariadne?"

56 31 [20] 1884–85; 11, 365

Also stand Zarathustra auf wie eine Morgensonne, die aus
den Bergen kommt: stark und glühend schreitet er daher—hin
zum großen Mittage, nach dem sein Wille begehrte, und hinab
zu seinem Untergange.

58 10 [45] 1883; 10, 377–78

I Act. Die Versuchungen. Er hält sich nicht für reif. (Aus-
gewähltes Volk)
Einsamkeit aus Scham vor sich

II Act. Zarathustra incognito dem „großen Mittage" bei-
wohnend
Wird erkannt

III. Act. Katastrophe: alle fallen ab nach seiner Rede.
Er stirbt vor Schmerz.

IV Act. Leichenfeier
„Wir tödteten ihn"
überredet die Gründe[6]

58   10 [46]

Zu 1). Er weigert sich. Endlich durch die Kinderchöre in Thränen.

Ein Narr!

2 Könige führen den Esel.

Zu 2) Als der Zug nicht weiß, wohin sich wenden, kommen die Gesandten aus der Peststadt. Entscheidung. Wie im W a l d. Feuer auf dem Markte symbol ⟨ische⟩ Reinigung.

Vernichtung der G r o ß s t a d t das Ende ich will die F r o m m e n verführen.

58   10 [47]

Zarathustra auf den Ruinen einer Kirche sitzend Act 4 der M i l d e s t e muß der H ä r t e s t e w e r d e n—und daran zu Grunde gehen.

Mild gegen den Menschen, hart um des Übermenschen willen

Collision.

anscheinende S c h w ä c h e.

er prophezeit ihnen: die Lehre der Wiederkehr ist das Z e i c h e n.

Er **vergißt sich** und lehrt **aus dem** Ü b e r m e n s c h e n **heraus** die Wiederkehr: der Übermensch h ä l t s i e a u s und z ü c h t i g t d a m i t.

Bei der Rückkehr aus der Vision stirbt er daran

60   13 [1] 1883; *10*, 443

(. . .)

„So will ich gerne sterben! Und abermals sterben! Und leben, um also zu sterben!" Und noch indem sie starb, lächelte sie: denn sie liebte Zarathustra.

Ein Gewitter murrte vom Himmel, unsichtbar noch.

Da erscholl ein Donner: und darauf kam eine Stille—wie mit furchtbaren Ringeln umwand und band uns diese Stille: die Welt stand still.

Dann verkündet das Weib das Kommen von Adler und Schlange. Das Zeichen. Allgemeine Flucht. Die Pest.

Sie zog den Arm Zarathustras an ihre Brust.

Und wiederum geschah das Athmen des Abgrundes: er stöhnte und brüllte sein Feuer herauf.
(. . .)

60   13 [2] 1883; *10*, 444–45
    1 Act. Zarathustra unter Thieren. Die Höhle.
            Das Kind mit dem Spiegel. (Es ist Zeit!)
            Die verschiedenen Anfragen, sich steigernd. Zuletzt
            verführen ihn die Kinder mit Gesang.
    2 Act. Die Stadt, Ausbruch der Pest. Aufzug Zarathustra's,
            Heilung des Weibes. Frühling.
    3 Act. Mittag und Ewigkeit.
    4 Act. Die Schiffer.
            Scene am Vulkan, Zarathustra unter Kindern
            sterbend.
            Todtenfeier.

                    Vorzeichen.
    zu 3.) Zarathustra sah und hörte nichts, er war entzückt.
            Dann schrittweise zurück in das furchtbarste Wissen.
    Die Empörung der Jünger, Fortgehen der Liebsten, Zara-
    thustra sucht sie zu halten. Die Schlange züngelt nach ihm.
    Er widerruft, Übermaß des Mitleidens, der Adler flieht.
    Jetzt die Scene des Weibes, an dem wieder die Pest aus-
    bricht. Aus Mitleid tödtet er. Er umarmt den Leichnam.
            Darauf das Schiff und die Erscheinung am Vulkan.
    „Zarathustra geht zur Hölle? Oder will er nun die Unterwelt
    erlösen?" — So verbreitet sich das Gerücht, er sei auch der
    Böse.
            Letzte Scene am Vulkan. Volle Seligkeit. Vergessen.
    Vision des Weibes (oder des Kindes mit dem Spiegel) Die
    Jünger schauen in das tiefe Grab. (Oder Zarathustra un-
    ter **Kindern** an Tempelresten.)
            Die größte aller Todtenfeiern macht den Schluß. Gol-
    dener Sarg in den Vulkan gestürzt.

61   13 [3] 1883; *10*, 446–47
        (. . .)
        Als er aber seine Schlange gegen sich züngeln sah, da verwand-
        elte sich langsam, langsam sein Gesicht: widerwillig sprang ihm
        das Thor der Erkenntniß auf: wie ein Blitz flog es hinein in die
        Tiefen seines Auges und wieder wie ein Blitz: es fehlte noch ein
        Augenblick, und er hätte gewußt— —Als das Weib diese Ver-
        wandlung sah, schrie es auf wie aus der höchsten Noth. „Stirb
        Zarathustra" —
        Mit seiner Linken drängte er den Adler zurück, der gegen ihn
        mit dem Ungestüm seiner Flügel schlug: er schrie, wie einer der
        zur Flucht räth; gern hätte er ihn davon getragen. Zu seiner
        Rechten auf dem Tische die Felsplatte
        (. . .)

62   16 [45] 1883; *10*, 513
        Als alle fort sind, streckt Zarathustra nach der Schlange die
        Hand aus: „was räth mir meine Klugheit?"—sie sticht ihn. Der
        Adler zerreißt sie, der Löwe stürzt sich über den Adler. Als
        Zarathustra den Kampf seiner Thiere sah, starb er.

62   13 [3] 1883; *10*, 446
        (. . .)
        „Du weißt es doch, Pana mein Kind, mein Sternlein, mein
        Goldohr—du weißt es doch, daß auch ich dich lieb habe?"
        Die Liebe zu mir hat dich überredet, ich sehe es: aber noch ver-
        stehe ich den Willen deiner Liebe nicht, Pana!—
        (. . .)

62   13 [3] 1883; *10*, 447
        (. . .)
        „Und was soll ich mit deinem Messer thun, Pana? Soll ich die gel-
        ben Trauben vom Weinstock schneiden? Siehe, welche Fülle um
        mich ist!"
        (. . .)

62   16 [38] 1883; *10*, 512
        Als er Pana erräth, stirbt Zarathustra vor Mitleid mit ihrem

Mitleid. Vorher der Augenblick der großen Verachtung (höchste Seligkeit!)

Alles muß in Erfüllung gehn, namentlich alles aus der V o r r e d e.

62   13 [1] 1883; *10*, 437

Ich rühre nicht an ihre Seele: und bald werde ich nicht einmal mehr ihre Haut erreichen.[7] Die letzte kleinste Kluft ist am schwersten zu überbrücken. That ich nicht euch am wehsten, als ich mir am liebsten that?

63   13 [3] 1883; *10*, 449 (cf. 366)

Nun steht nur noch die kleinste Kluft zwischen mir und dir: aber wehe! Wer schlug je eine Brücke über die kleinsten Klüfte?

63   16 [3] 1883; *10*, 495–96

In Act II kommen die verschiedenen Gruppen und bringen ihr Geschenk. „Was thatet ihr?"—Sie sagen es.—„So ist es aus dem Geiste Zarathustras gethan."

Die Lehre der Wiederkunft wird zuerst das Gesindel anlächeln, das kalt und ohne viel innere Noth ist. Der gemeinste Lebenstrieb giebt zuerst seine Zustimmung. **Eine große Wahrheit gewinnt sich zuallerletzt die höchsten Menschen:** d i e s i s t d a s L e i d e n d e r W a h r h a f t i g e n.

Act I. Einsamkeit aus Scham vor sich: E i n u n a u s g e s p r o c h - e n e r G e d a n k e, d e m e r s i c h z u s c h w a c h f ü h l t (z u w e n i g h a r t) D i e V e r s u c h u n g e n, i h n d a r ü b e r z u t ä u s c h e n. Die Boten des ausgewählten Volks laden ihn zum Feste des Lebens.

Act II. Er wohnt incognito dem Feste bei. Er verräth sich, als er sich zu geehrt findet.

Act III. Im Glück verkündet er den Übermenschen und dessen Lehre. Alle fallen ab. Er stirbt, als die Vision ihn verläßt, vor Schmerz darüber, welches Leid er geschaffen.

T o d t e n f e i e r. „Wir tödteten ihn"—Mittag und Ewigkeit.

65   16 [55] 1883; *10*, 518

Plan zum 4. Zarathustra.

1. Der Sieges-Zug, die Pest-Stadt, der symbolische Scheiterhaufen. 30
2. Die Verkündungen der Zukunft: seine Schüler erzählen
   ihre Thaten. 30
3. Die letzte Rede mit Vorzeichen, Unterbrechungen, Re-
   gen, Tod. 30
4. Der Bund auf seinem Grabe — die Gelobenden — der
   große Mittag — ahnungsvoll-heiter und schauerlich. 30

65   16 [65] 1883; *10*, 522–23
Der dritte Theil ist die Selbst-Überwindung Zarathustras, als
Vorbild der Selbst-Überwindung der Menschheit — zu Gunst-
en des Übermenschen.

Dazu ist die Überwindung der Moral nöthig.

Du opferst deine Freunde — sie sind tief genug, um dran
zu Grunde zu gehn: und sie haben den Gedanken nicht geschaffen (was mich noch hält!)

Dies als letztes Gegen-Argument, welches sich Zarathustra
entgegenstellt — der stärkste Feind. Jetzt wird Zarathustra reif.

Im Theil 4 stirbt Zarathustra, als er den Schmerz seiner
Freunde merkt: und sie ihn verlassen. — Aber nach seinem
Tode kommt sein Geist über sie.
(. . .)

66   20 [10] 1883; *10*, 593–94[8]
                  Zarathustra 4.
Der König und der Narr geben einen Begriff, daß das Kommen
Zarathustra's nöthig ist.

Zarathustra schließt immer engere Kreise: große Reden, worin
er ausschließt. Immer kleinere Kreise, auf höheren Bergen.

Zunächst werden 1) die Schmarotzer, dann 2) die Heuchler 3)
die Schwachen Gutmüthigen dann 4) die unbewußten Heuchler
der Moral ausgeschlossen.

Letzte Scene: Schilderung der höchsten Seele, die am Tief-
sten hinunter kann, der umfänglichsten, die sich am weitesten
verirren kann, der nothwendigsten, die sich in Zufälle stürzt, der
Seienden, die ins Werden sich verliebt; der Habenden, welche

verlangt und will; der sich immer wieder Fliehenden und wieder Einholenden: ganz Selbst-Liebe und darum ganz in Allem: der alles Spiel ist; Weisheit, die sich ins Meer der Thorheit stürzt: Lachen und Tränen: die Welt, eines Gottes Ausgelassenheit: Erlösung von allen einmaligen steifen „Weisen." usw. — Sünde selber als Genuß der Selbst-Aufhebung.

Alle Wesen nur **Vorübungen** in der Vereinigung **Einverleibung** von Gegensätzen.

Die Erlösung vom Zufalle: was ich habe geschehen lassen, das weiß ich hinterdrein **mir gut machen**: und deshalb hinterdrein wollen, was ich nicht vorher wollte.

ganz in sich Ziel

Darauf erzählt Zarathustra, aus dem Glück des Übermenschen heraus, das **Geheimniß** daß Alles wiederkehrt.

Wirkung. Pana will ihn tödten.

Er begreift endlich, macht alle Wandlungen durch, bis zur siegreichsten, als er aber sie zerbrochen liegen sieht — lacht. Steigt lachend aufwärts auf den Fels: aber dort angekommen stirbt er glücklich.

Hinreißende Wirkung des Todes: die Gelobenden.

67   21 [3] 1883; *10*, 598–600

Plan zu Zarathustra 4.

1. Die Einladung.
2. Der Siegeszug. Die Peststadt. Der Scheiterhaufen (die alte Cultur verbrannt).
3. Das Frühlingsfest mit Chören.
4. Rechenschaft vor Zarathustra: „was thatet ihr?" (erfandet ihr?)

(. . .)

9. das Weib im Weibe erlösen

(. . .)

21. **Entscheidender Moment:** Zarathustra fragt die ganze Masse am Feste: „wollt ihr das Alles noch einmal?" — alles sagt „Ja!"

Er stirbt vor Glück dabei.

(der Himmel heiter, tief)

(ahnungsvoll, heiter, schauerlich)

(tiefste Stille, die Thiere um Zarathustra, er hat das Haupt verhüllt, die Arme über die Felsplatte gebreitet — scheint zu schlafen)
der heulende Hund
etwas Leuchtendes Furchtbares Stilles geht ihnen allen über ihre Gedanken weg
Den Schluß bilden die Reden der Gelobenden an seiner Leiche.

Die Gelobenden.

22. usw. Der große Mittag als Wendepunkt — die zwei Wege. Der Hammer zur Überwältigung des Menschen: höchste Entfaltung des Individuums, so daß es an sich zu Grunde gehen muß (und nicht, wie bisher, an Diätfehlern!) (wie der Tod in die Welt kam!)
Was Glück![9]
Der Schaffende als der Selbst-Vernichter. Schöpfer aus Güte und Weisheit. Alle bisherige Moral überboten!
Zuletzt die Gelöbnisse — furchtbare Schwüre!

68   29 [15] 1884–85; *11*, 341
   der sterbende Zarathustra hält die Erde umarmt. — Und obgleich es Niemand ihnen gesagt hatte, wußten sie alle, daß Zarathustra todt war.

68   34 [144] 1885; *11*, 468
   NB. — er bewegte und schloß wieder die Lippen und blickte wie Einer, der noch etwas zu sagen hat und zögert es zu sagen. Und es dünkte denen, welche ihm zusahen, daß sein Gesicht dabei leise eröthet sei. Dies dauerte eine kleine Weile: dann aber, mit Einem Male, schüttelte er den Kopf, schloß freiwillig die Augen — und starb. —
   Also geschah, daß Zarathustra untergieng.

71   35 [73] 1885; *11*, 541
   I. Zarathustra kann nur beglücken, nachdem die Rangordnung hergestellt ist. Zunächst wird diese gelehrt.
   II. Die Rangordnung durchgeführt in einem System der Erdregierung: die Herrn der Erde zuletzt, eine neue herr-

schende Kaste. Aus ihnen hier und da entspringend, ganz epicurischer Gott, der Übermensch, der Verklärer des Daseins.

III. Die übermenschliche Auffassung der Welt. Dionysos.

IV. Von dieser größten Entfremdung liebend zurückkehrend zum Engsten und Kleinsten, Zarathustra alle seine Erlebnisse segnend und als Segnender sterbend.

72   35 [75] 1885; *11*, 542

1. Zarathustra auf der alten Festung erwachend. Hört die Trommeln der Herolde.
2. Die Prüfung: „Gehört ihr zu mir?"
3. Der Rosenfest-Zug.
4. Die Lehre von der Rangordnung.
5. Nachts an der Brücke.

72   39 [3] 1885; *11*, 620

Zarathustra 5 (die Jugend als Grundton)
                    kriegerisch im höchsten Grade
Auf einer alten Festung die Trommeln der Herolde.
            (Finale) des Nachts wie am Rialto.
                    das Rosenfest.

Zarathustra der gottlose Einsiedler, der erste Einsame, der nicht betete.

Seid ihr jetzt stark genug für meine Wahrheiten?

Wer gehört zu mir?   was ist vornehm?

„Seid ihr Solche?" (als Refrain) die Rangordnung: und ihr müßt alles in euch haben, um herrschen zu können, aber auch unter euch!

Refrain: und wenn ihr nicht sprechen dürft: „wir ehren sie, doch sind wir höherer Art" — so seid ihr nicht von meiner Art.

Das Rosenfest.

Nachts an der Brücke.

(. . .)

73   39 [22] 1885; *11*, 628

(. . .)

Zarathustra auf den Wällen der Festung gehend: — er hört

den absoluten Pessimismus predigen. Die Stadt wird umringt.
Er schweigt.

73   1 [162] 1885–86; *12*, 47–48
                    Die orgiastische Seele.—
Ich habe ihn gesehn: seine Augen wenigstens — es sind bald
tiefe stille, bald grüne und schlüpfrige Honig-Augen
    sein halkyonisches Lächeln,
    der Himmel sah blutig und grausam zu

                die orgiastische Seele des Weibes
    ich habe ihn gesehn, sein halkyonisches Lächeln, seine
Honig-Augen, bald tief und verhüllt, bald grün und schlüpfrig,
eine zitternde Oberfläche,

        schlüpfrig, schläfrig, zitternd, zaudernd,
        quillt die See in seinen Augen

73   1 [163]
        1. Cäsar unter Seeräubern
        2. An der Brücke
        3. Die Hochzeit. — und plötzlich, während der Himmel
                                dunkel herniederfällt
        4. Ariadne.

73   1 [164]
        Diese Musik—doch dionysisch?
        der Tanz?
        die Heiterkeit? der Versucher?
        die religiöse Fluth?
        unter Platos Kopfkissen Ar⟨istophanes⟩?

73   1 [165]
        unsre Spielleute und M⟨enschen⟩ des unehrlichen Begräb-
        nisses—es sind die Nächstverwandten der Hexen, sie haben ihre
        Blocksberge

73   1 [166]
        die mystische Natur, durch Laster besudelt und schäumend

73   1 [167]

die gütige und reine Quelle, die niemals mehr mit einem Trop-
fen Unraths fertig wird der in sie fiel, bis sie endlich gelb und giftig
durch und durch ist:—die verderbten Engel

78   2 [129] 1885–86; *12*, 128–29

Die ewige Wiederkunft.

Zarathustrische Tänze und
Umzüge.
Erster Theil: Gottes Todtenfest.

Von
Friedrich Nietzsche.

1. Gottes Todtenfest.
2. Am großen Mittag.
3. „Wo ist die Hand für diesen Hammer?"
4. Wir Gelobenden.

I.

Die Peststadt. Er wird gewarnt, er fürchtet sich nicht und geht
hinein, verhüllt. Alle Arten des Pessimismus ziehen vorbei. Der
Wahrsager d e u t e t jeden Zug. Die Sucht zum Anders, die Sucht
zum Nein, endlich die Sucht zum Nichts folgen sich.

Zuletzt giebt Zarathustra die E r k l ä r u n g: Gott ist todt, dies ist
die U r s a c h e der größten Gefahr: wie? sie könnte auch die Ur-
sache des größten Muths sein!

II.

Das Erscheinen der Freunde.

Der Genuß der Untergehenden an d e m V o l l k o m m e n e n:
Abziehende.

Die Rechenschaft der Freunde.

Festzüge. Die entscheidende Zeit, der große Mittag.

Das große Dank- und Todtenopfer an den todten Gott.

III.

Die neue Aufgabe.   Der Tod Gottes, für den

Das Mittel der Aufgabe.   Wahrsager das furchtbarste Er-
Die Freunde verlassen ihn.   eigniß, ist das Glücklichste und
                              Hoffnungs reichste für Zarathustra.
       Zarathustra stirbt.

IV. Wir Gelobenden

79   2 [71] 1885–86; *12*, 93–94
        Zum „Zarathustra".

        Calina: braunroth, alles zu scharf in der Nähe. Höchste
Sonne. Gespenstisch.

        Sipo Matador.

        Und wer sagt es, daß wir dies nicht wollen? Welche Musik und
Verführung! Da ist nichts, das nicht vergiftete, verlockte, an-
nagte, umwürfe, umwerthete!

        I Der entscheidende Moment:
        Die Rangordnung.   1) Zerbrecht die Guten und
                                    Gerechten!
                             2)
        Die ewige Wiederkunft.

                Mittag und Ewigkeit.
                Buch des Wahrsagers.

79   2 [72]

                Mittag und Ewigkeit.
                     Von
                     F. N.

        I   Das Todtenfest. Zarathustra findet ein ungeheures Fest vor:
        II Die neue Rangordnung.
        III Von den Herrn der Erde.
        IV Vom Ring der Wiederkunft.

80   28 [32–33] 1884; *11*, 312–13
        (. . .)

24 Calina braunroth, alles zu scharf in der Nähe
im höchsten Sommer. Gespenstisch (meine jetzige Gefahr!)
(. . .)

11 Calina: meine jetzige Gefahr, im höchsten Sommer,
gespenstisch, braun-roth, alles zu scharf in der Nähe
(. . .)

81   9 [115] 1887; *12*, 401–02

(. . .)
Satyrspiel
am Schluß
Einmischen: kurze Gespräche zwischen Theseus Dionysos
und Ariadne.

—Theseus wird absurd, sagte Ariadne, Theseus wird tugend-
haft—
Eifersucht des Theseus auf Ariadne's Traum.
Der Held sich selbst bewundernd, absurd werdend.   Klage der
Ariadne[10]
Dionysos ohne Eifersucht: „Was ich an Dir liebe, wie könnte das
ein Theseus lieben?" . . .
Letzter Akt. Hochzeit des Dionysos und der Ariadne
„man ist nicht eifersüchtig, wenn man Gott ist, sagte Dionysos:
es sei denn auf Götter."

   „Ariadne, sagte Dionysos, du bist ein Labyrinth: Theseus hat
sich in dich verirrt, er hat keinen Faden mehr; was nützt es ihm
nun, daß er nicht vom Minotauros gefressen wurde? Was ihn
frißt, ist schlimmer als ein Minotauros." Du schmeichelst mir,
antwortete Ariadne, aber ich bin meines Mitleidens müde, an
mir sollen alle Helden zu Grunde gehen: das ist meine letzte Liebe
zu Theseus: „ich richte ihn zu Grunde"

83   20 [127] 1888; *13*, 570
ein Gedanke,
jetzt noch heiß-flüssig, Lava:
aber jede Lava baut
um sich selbst eine Burg,

jeder Gedanke erdrückt
sich zuletzt mit "Gesetzen"

84   20 [128] 1888; *13*, 570
als keine neue Stimme mehr redete,
machtet ihr aus alten Worten
ein Gesetz:
wo Leben e r s t a r r t, thürmt sich das Gesetz.

84   20 [48] 1888; *13*, 557–58
Die Wahrheit—
ein Weib, nichts Besseres:
arglistig in ihrer Scham:
was sie am liebsten möchte,
sie will's nicht wissen,
sie hält die Finger vor. . .
Wem giebt sie nach? Der Gewalt allein!—
So braucht Gewalt,
seid hart, ihr Weisesten!
ihr müßt sie zwingen
die verschämte Wahrheit. . .
zu ihrer Seligkeit
braucht's des Zwanges—
—sie ist ein Weib, nicht⟨s⟩ Besseres . . .

NOTES

Introduction: "It's the Women!"

1. Jacques Derrida, *Éperons: Les styles de Nietzsche* (Paris: Garnier-Flammarion, 1978), p. 82. The French text and an English translation by Barbara Harlow appear *en face* in Derrida, *Spurs: Nietzsche's Styles* (Chicago: University of Chicago Press, 1979). I shall cite both editions in my text, as follows: (82/100).

2. Nietzsche had planned (see *12*, 82–86) to devote an entire section of *Beyond Good and Evil* to "Woman in Itself," *Das Weib an sich.* The section was jettisoned in favor of "Maxims and Entr'actes" and aphorisms 231–39 of "Our Virtues." See Nietzsche's letter to C. Heymons of April 12, 1886; see also *11*, 229.

3. Derrida's fascination with Nietzsche's sails may have been stimulated by Jacques Lacan's "L'instance de la lettre"; see Lacan, *Écrits* (Paris: Seuil, 1966), pp. 505–06. See also Bernard Pautrat, *Versions du soleil: Figures et système de Nietzsche* (Paris: Seuil, 1971), pp. 48–122.

4. See *Spurs*, pp. 32 and 103 ff. (pp. 40 and 122 ff.); the reference in Nietzsche is to 12 [62] 1881 (*9*, 587). What hermeneutics could never do, however, René Magritte has done: see Krell, "The End of Metaphysics: Hegel and Nietzsche on Holiday," in *Research in Phenomenology*, XIII (1983), pp. 175–82. See also Nietzsche's diagram in 22 [17] 1877; *8*, 382. For a more detailed account of Derrida's *Spurs*, see Krell, "A Hermeneutics of Discretion," *Research in Phenomenology*, XV (1985), pp. 1–27.

5. Derrida's aversion to the in-itself gains support from Nietzsche's own remarks in "The Advantage and Disadvantage of History for Life" (UB II, 5; *1*, 279–85). Here Nietzsche's prevailing metaphor for the historian is the *eunuch* who has been charged with the task of keeping in order the harem of world history. "To the eunuch, one woman is like another, merely a woman, *das Weib an sich*, eternally unapproachable" (*1*, 284). To the historian, polymorphously anaesthetized, the "candid, naked goddess Philosophy" is of no interest. The literary critic fares slightly better in Nietzsche's account, inasmuch as his castration is purely symbolic: his is the general debility of the modern personality—his "critical ejaculations" are ceaseless; he lacks self-control; his vast superfluity is a sign of *impotentia*.

6. In addition to Derrida's remarks on pp. 32–33 (p. 42) of *Spurs*, see Jacques Derrida, *L'oreille de l'autre*, eds. Claude Lévesque and Christie V. McDonald (Montreal: VLB Éditeur, 1982), esp. pp. 11–56, "Otobiographie de Nietzsche," keeping in the mind's ear these words from the *Oxford English Dictionary*: "Oto-, . . . ear, an element of medical and other scientific words [such as] Otography, description of the ear." Not to mention Fundamental Otology, study of the unifold invagination of *Dasein*, site of the ultimate vulnerability: Claudius' poison, according to Hamlet père, was poured "in the porches of mine ears," and by the deceptions of Claudius, that incestuous and adulterous beast, "the whole ear of Denmark/ Is . . . rankly abus'd" (I, 5). See also "tympan," in Derrida, *Marges de la philosophie* (Paris: Minuit, 1972), esp. pp. iv–xiii. See now also Derrida, *Otobiographies* (Paris: Editions Galilée, 1984).

7. Derrida would have been intrigued to find an earlier use of the image *inmitten einer Brandung*, in *Daybreak* (*3*, 239); here it communicates the experience of shame, an experience made famous by Sartre's description of *le regard*. Nietzsche writes: "*Center. The*

feeling that 'I am the midpoint of the world!' rises very strongly in us whenever we are suddenly overcome by shame; we stand there as though anaesthetized in the midst of a surf; we feel ourselves to be dazzled by an enormous eye that gazes on us, through us, from all sides." For another use of the surf image, see *10*, 497.

    8. See esp. JGB, 257 (*5*, 205); ZGM I, 2 (*5*, 259); and ZGM III, 14 (*5*, 371).

    9. On "space" in Plato, see Krell, "Female Parts in *Timaeus*," in *Arion: A Journal of Humanities and the Classics* (New Series, No. 2, 1975), 400–21, esp. 412–14. On "undistancing," *Ent-fernung*, see Martin Heidegger, *Sein und Zeit*, 12th ed. (Tübingen: M. Niemeyer, 1972), section 23. Being as *Entzug* and *Ereignis/Enteignis* are discussed in many places. See esp. *Zur Sache des Denkens* (Tübingen: M. Niemeyer, 1969), pp. 44, 53, and 58. Note Derrida's discussion in *Spurs*, pp. 38–39 and 95–102 (pp. 48–50 and 114–22).

    10. See *Wegmarken* (Frankfurt am Main: V. Klostermann, 1967), "Vom Wesen der Wahrheit," sections 6–7.

    11. *Spurs*, pp. 47 ff. (pp. 60 ff.). See also *La carte postale* (Paris: Garnier-Flammarion, 1980), pp. 439–524, along with the earlier Derridean texts cited there on p. 448 n. 2. An excellent source for Lacanian theory is Jacques Lacan and the École Freudienne, *Feminine Sexuality*, eds. Juliet Mitchell and Jacqueline Rose (London: Macmillan, 1982). Derrida's reply to Lacan in *La carte postale*, so unsatisfying as regards the crucial question of *desire*, requires a careful reading of Lacan, *Écrits*, esp. pp. 11–61; 493–528; and 855–77.

    12. See *Spurs*, p. 75 n. 1 (pp. 148–50) and p. 89 (p. 108). The themes introduced here are pursued in Jacques Derrida, "*Geschlecht*: Différence sexuelle, différence ontologique," in *Heidegger*, ed. Michel Haar (Paris: Cahiers de L'Herne, 1983), pp. 419–30. An English translation appears in *Research in Phenomenology*, XIII (1983), pp. 65–83. See also Christie V. McDonald's interview with Derrida, "Choreographies," in *Diacritics*, XII (Summer 1982), pp. 66–76, and Verena Andermatt Conley's correspondence with him in *Boundary 2*, XII, 2 (Winter 1984), 68–93. Perhaps it is not too fanciful to suggest that a number of Derrida's remarks here are responses to a remarkable book (recommended to me by a reader for Indiana University Press, to whom I here express my gratitude): Luce Irigaray's *Amante marine: de Friedrich Nietzsche* (Paris: Editions de Minuit, 1980). In the second part of her book, "Lèvres voilées," Irigaray (see esp. pp. 110–18) reproduces those Nietzschean texts taken up into Derrida's *Spurs* that I have been considering here. While appearing to make use of Derrida's deconstruction of (male) "essentializing fetishes," Irigaray nonetheless insists on maintaining the definite article(s): *l'homme*, bearer of the rigid, cadaverous phallus, veiler/violator of woman, congenitally incapable *as such* of embrace; *la femme*, sea lover, tongue and lips embracing without penetration, enjoying the most intense and innocent of pleasures outside all dismal economies of desire. Profound pleasure belongs to the "sub-sisters" alone who, disburdened of the phallus, combine in and for themselves (through "auto-affection") "prime matter" and pure "form" (91–92). Which leaves only the question as to why such bliss must express itself in the phallogocentric language and rigid binary oppositions of metaphysics.

Chapter One: Ariadne

    1. Karl Reinhardt, "Nietzsches Klage der Ariadne" has been reprinted in several collections in Germany, though I am aware of no English translation as yet. I cite the text as reproduced in Karl Reinhardt, *Vermächtnis der Antike: Gesammelte Essays zur Philosophie und Geschichtsschreibung*, ed. Carl Becker (Göttingen: Vandenhoek und Ruprecht, 1960), pp. 310–33. See also Reinhardt's less well-known but equally thought-provoking lecture, "Nietzsche und die Geschichte," pp. 296–309.

    2. See the notebooks collected under Mette-no. 28 (*11*, 297–332; cf. *14*, 708–16). The *Dithyrambs* themselves appear in *6*, 375–445; cf. *14*, 513–18.

3. The definitive remark on this beating is Nietzsche's own (JGB, 40; 5, 57–58): "There are occurrences of so delicate a kind that one does well to cover them over and disguise them behind something coarse; there are deeds of love and extravagant generosity after which nothing is more advisable than to take a stick and pummel the witness: that way you becloud his memory."

4. It is precisely here that Heidegger's 1937 lecture course ("Eternal Recurrence of the Same") makes reply. See esp. sections 4, 8, and 9 of M. Heidegger, *Nietzsche, Volume II: The Eternal Recurrence of the Same* (New York: Harper & Row, 1984), pp. 28–31 and 49–69.

5. See, for example, *Twilight of the Idols*, 6, 117–18.

6. Compare to *6*, 160 the much earlier statement, 8 [14] 1883, at *10*, 334–35.

7. Published in Paris by the Presses Universitaires de France in 1962. I shall cite this edition by page number in my text. An English translation by Hugh Tomlinson (London: Athlone Press, 1983) is now available.

8. Recall the "aria" sung by the earthshaker in *The Gay Science* (see pp. 6–7, above). It is just as well that Deleuze refuses to play, inasmuch as the aria of *Ari-ane* would be entertainment fit for a king—at the "Ass Festival" of *Thus Spoke Zarathustra*, Part IV. On the origins of the name *Ariadne-Ariagne*, see W. F. Otto, *Dionysos: Mythos und Kultus* (Frankfurt am Main: V. Klostermann, 1933), p. 166.

9. On the "spider," see Sarah Kofman, *Nietzsche et la métaphore* (Paris: Payot, 1972), pp. 101–06 which however does not take up the arachnoid thread of Ariadne. On the questions of woman, sensuality, and death in Nietzsche, see chapter 8 of Kofman, *Nietzsche et la scène philosophique* (Paris: Union Générale d'Editions, 10/18, 1979), pp. 265, 269–70, and 285–99.

10. See chapter 3, "Pana," p. 55, below. Luce Irigaray is eloquent in her rejection of merely "mirrored" affirmation; see *Amante marine*, pp. 60–62, 79, 125, 201, and elsewhere.

11. Bernard Pautrat, *Versions du soleil*, pp. 325–26, finds the figure of Ariadne most resistant to philosophical interpretation: she is the guiding thread of embodiment, of the human body as such, of overdetermination, excess, unconscious drives, and desire. Note also the importance of Ariadne and the Labyrinth for Eckhard Heftrich, *Nietzsches Philosophie: Identität von Welt und Nichts* (Frankfurt am Main: V. Klostermann, 1962), esp. Part I.

Chapter Two: Corinna

1. Compare with what follows the remarks by Bernard Pautrat in *Versions du soleil*: on renouncing the search for "pure" parents of tragedy, p. 87; on tragedy itself as the fold or pleat (*pli*) of bisexuality, pp. 118–20; and on Dionysos himself (?) as the mother of tragedy, *passim*.

2. The classic source for all such questions is of course Otto's *Dionysos: Mythos und Kultus*. On the question of Dionysos and woman, see esp. chapters 15 and 16. Yet Otto is so anxious to deny an assertive, aggressive sexuality of Dionysos that he winds up in a curiously inverted phallocentrism: he celebrates as the "genuinely female" nature the maternal traits of nurture—mothercare—and deprives woman of intense erotic desire (161–62). On the question of Dionysos' "oriental" character, see Edward Said, *Orientalism* (London: Routledge and Kegan Paul, 1978), pp. 56–57. Said says unfortunately all too little about this particular kind of orientalism.

3. Consider M, 75 (*3*, 72–73): "There is something female in Christianity, betrayed in the thought that 'whom God loves, He chastises'." In JGB, 46 (5, 66–67) Nietzsche refers to the "cruelty and religious Phoenicianism" of the Christian faith, rem-

iniscent of the "Sekaean orgies" of GT. When God is nailed to the Cross, "It is the Orient, the *deep* Orient, it is the Oriental slave taking vengeance on Rome and its aristocratic, frivolous tolerance, on the Roman 'catholicity' of belief." See also JGB, 50 (5, 70–71) for an account of Oriental ecstasy and the sexual nature of Christian mysticism.

4. See I. Kant, *Anthropology from a Pragmatic Point of View*, on "the sensible imagination of affinity" (Akademie Ausgabe, pp. 177–78n.):

> One could call the first two kinds of combinations of representations [i.e., *imaginatio plastica* and *imaginatio assozians*] the *mathematical* kinds (having to do with enlargement); but one could call the third kind [i.e., *affinitas, Verwandtschaft*] the dynamic (having to do with generation [*Erzeugung*]), whereby an entirely new thing (somewhat like a salt in chemistry) is produced. The play of forces—in lifeless nature as well as in animate nature, in the soul as well as in the body—rests on dissolutions and unifications of dissimilars. True, we attain knowledge of these whenever we experience their effects; yet their highest cause and the simple components into which their matter can be resolved are beyond our reach. —What might be the cause of the fact that all known organic creatures reproduce their kind solely by means of the unification of two sexes (which one then calls the male and the female)? Surely we cannot assume that the Creator, merely on account of some eccentricity and simply in order to devise an arrangement on our earthly globe that pleased Him, was only playing, as it were; rather, it seems that it must be *impossible* to enable organic creatures to originate from the matter on our globe through reproduction in any other way, without there having been founded two sexes to that end. —In what obscurity does human reason lose itself when it undertakes even by way of surmise to ground here its lineage [*den Abstamm zu ergründen*]?

A question one might trace with advantage through the Enlightenment, Romanticism-Idealism, and Nietzsche (who calls Kant's "obscurity" an "abyss of thought"), into the groping twentieth century.

5. Nietzsche's early autobiographical materials do not appear in the Colli-Montinari critical edition. See the edition by Karl Schlechta (Munich: C. Hanser, 1956), III, 96. Curt Paul Janz (*Friedrich Nietzsche: Biographie* [Munich: Deutscher Taschenbuch Verlag, 1981], I, 78–80), is right to acknowledge how rare and perceptive such admiration of Hölderlin is prior to World War I; he cites the teacher's response to Nietzsche's essay: "I would like to offer the author some friendly advice: stick to a healthier, more lucid, and more German poet." Yet Janz is mistaken when he says that no trace of an influence can be ascertained in the case of Hölderlin's and Nietzsche's respective Empedocles fragments. The word *Wiederkehr*, a persistent refrain in Hölderlin's text, should make us more cautious. It is nonetheless true that whereas Hölderlin *reduces* the role of woman with each successive draft, Nietzsche *enhances* it: Corinna will become what Panthea never was.

6. Hölderlin composed the "Frankfurt Plan" in the summer of 1797. See *Hölderlin Werke und Briefe*, ed. Friedrich Beissner and Jochen Schmidt (Frankfurt am Main: Insel Verlag, 1969), II, 567. I have been unable to discover any indication that Nietzsche knew of Matthew Arnold's magnificent *Empedocles on Etna*, first published in 1852, then suppressed by the author in the 1853 edition of his *Poems*. Arnold suppressed the play because of its dispiriting quality, the failure of its suffering to find a "vent in action." Arnold's retrospect on the play is highly reminiscent of Hölderlin's "Plan" and foreshadows much in Nietzsche's treatment of the same subject. In the Preface to the 1853 *Poems* Arnold writes: "I intended to delineate the feelings of one of the last of the Greek religious philosophers, one of the family of Orpheus and Musaeus, having survived his fellows, living on into a time when the habits of Greek thought and feeling had begun fast to change, character to dwindle, the influence of the Sophists to prevail. Into the feelings of a man so situated there entered much that we are accustomed to consider as exclusively modern; how much,

the fragments of Empedocles himself which remain to us are sufficient at least to indicate. What those who are familiar only with the great monuments of early Greek genius suppose to be its exclusive characteristics, have disappeared; the calm, the cheerfulness, the disinterested objectivity have disappeared: the dialogue of the mind with itself has commenced; modern problems have presented themselves; we hear already the doubts, we witness the discouragement, of Hamlet and of Faust." Arnold thus confirms the modernity, and perhaps even the futurity, of the ancient physician of culture. See *The Poems of Matthew Arnold*, ed. Miriam Allott (London: Longman, 1979), p. 654. —I am grateful to Gabriel Pearson for giving me Arnold to read.

7. See, for example, 7, 43. In "Schopenhauer as Educator" (UB III; *1*, 361) Nietzsche argues that "for ages hence it will be important to know what Empedocles asserted of existence," namely, his total affirmation of it. Empedocles is the "masterful, creative man." He bears the attributes that will later be ascribed to Zarathustra: he is the "advocate" and "redeemer" of existence. Yet Empedocles' answer to the question of existence, his total affirmation, is irremediably tragic. It echoes in the crater of Etna. In *Human, All-Too-Human* (no. 141; *2*, 135) Nietzsche stresses the *erotic* nature of Empedoclean advocacy. "In all pessimistic religions the act of procreation is felt to be base in itself; yet this feeling is by no means universal among human beings. Not even the judgment of all pessimists is the same in this regard. Empedocles, for example, recognizes nothing shameful, demonic, or sinful in any erotic matters. In the vast meadow of misery he sees but one medicinal, hope-dispensing appearance: Aphrodite. She alone serves as guarantor of the fact that conflict does not prevail eternally, that the scepter is finally handed on to a milder daimon." Finally, compare Nietzsche's account of *Parmenidean* Aphrodite (as cited in Fr. 12) in *Philosophy in the Tragic Age of the Greeks*, section 9 (*1*, 838–39).

8. As philological fate would have it, the Colli-Montinari *Kritische Gesamtausgabe* does not contain such lecture material, inasmuch as it pertains to Nietzsche's *philologica*. See the *Grossoktavausgabe* (Leipzig: A. Kröner, 1913), XIX, 189–201.

9. Gaston Bachelard comments on this passage: "So why did Nietzsche report that 'Empedocles remembered being . . . boy and girl'? Does this astonish Nietzsche? Doesn't he see in this Empedoclean memory a token of the depth of meditation of one of the heroes of thought? . . . Does this text help us descend into the unfathomable depths of the human? . . . Is it by reliving the times when the philosopher was 'boy-girl' that we shall discover a line of inquiry for 'analyzing' the virility of the super-human? Ah! really what are philosophers dreaming of?" See *The Poetics of Reverie*, tr. Daniel Russell (Boston: Beacon Press, 1969), p. 59.

10. For the first group of plans see 5 [116–18] 1870–71; 7, 125–26. For the second group see 8 [30–37] 1871–72; 7, 233–37. For the third, 9 [4] 1871; 7, 269–71. Perhaps the only interesting feature of the third plan is the fact that "Corinna" there becomes an aged noblewoman—who has a daughter called "Lesbia."

11. Nietzsche himself had access to S. Karsten, *Philosophorum Graecorum Veterum . . . Operum Reliquiae* (1835), as did Matthew Arnold. (Nietzsche cites Karsten, for example, in his lecture notes: *Grossoktavausgabe*, XIX, 193–94.) Karsten (ii 24–25) reports as follows: "So there is said to have been a woman of Acragas, whose name they also record—Hermippus reported that she was called Pantheia—who had stayed several continuous days . . . without breath or heartbeat, differing from a corpse only in that some heat remained around the middle of her body. Empedocles restored the life, breath and health of this woman, who had been given up by doctors and mourned for dead." Cited in *Poems of Matthew Arnold*, pp. 160–61.

12. Hölderlin himself uses the word *Wiederkehr*, "recurrence," as well as *Wiedergeburt*, "rebirth." (See the Insel edition, II, 500, 536–37, and 560.) Empedoclean rebirth

will not become eternal recurrence until a decade has elapsed; but woman, as nature, will have been abiding all the while. Reverting to the earlier point: the Faustian character of this note becomes apparent when we read a sketch that appears several pages before the *Empedocles* plans (7, 118): "Empedocles is the purely tragic human being. His leap into Etna occurs because of—the drive to knowledge! He longed for art, yet found only knowledge. But knowledge makes Fausts." The last phrase suggests both that the drive to knowledge is Faustian and that it is threatening: *jemandem Fäuste machen* means to threaten with fists. And Dionysian excess? The next three lines of the note read: "The festival and the tragic worldview./ The tragic woman./ Sexual love in tragedy."

Chapter Three: Pana

1. See *Nietzsche* (Pfullingen: G. Neske, 1961), I, 323; English translation, Volume II, p. 67.

2. Curt Paul Janz (II, 223–24) cites the influence of the Empedocles motif not only on the planned Zarathustran drama but also on the book *Thus Spoke Zarathustra* itself. "Even though Nietzsche did not choose *Empedocles* as the title of his work, this Presocratic figure and his legacy nonetheless hover over Nietzsche's impressions: the intertwining of natural science, Ionian nature philosophy, and Pythagorean-Eleatic mysticism." Janz stresses the importance of this early Greek influence on the *form* and *style* of *Zarathustra* as well. He records that the very first commentary on the book, that of Gustav Naumann, from the years 1899–1901, drew attention to these matters, "seeing in Nietzsche's *Empedocles* fragment nothing less than the prototype of Zarathustra." Finally, Janz elsewhere (II, 381–82) speculates that the plans we are about to examine reflect Nietzsche's failure to achieve for Zarathustra a *telos* "such as Empedocles had found," that is, a death that would express a particular doctrine and way of life.

3. See the final chapter of Wolfgang Müller-Lauter, *Nietzsche: Seine Philosophie der Gegensätze und die Gegensätze seiner Philosophie* (Berlin: W. de Gruyter, 1971), which distinguishes two very different kinds of *Übermensch* and eternal return.

4. See Krell, "Descensional Reflection," in *Philosophy and Archaic Experience: Essays in Honor of Edward G. Ballard*, ed. John Sallis (Pittsburgh: Duquesne University Press, 1982), pp. 3–12; and "Der Maulwurf/The Mole," in *Why Nietzsche Now?*, ed. Daniel O'Hara (Bloomington: Indiana University Press, 1985), pp. 155–85.

5. See *Sein und Zeit*, p. 264. Note that Nietzsche himself employs the phrase *Freiheit zum Tode* in 1 [43] 1882 (*10*, 21).

6. The third section of this song bears the title *Dionysos* in the manuscript. In it occurs the "toss of the dice" that so captures the imagination of Gilles Deleuze. The sixth section too radiates the Dionysian hue, is all "emerald-gold" (*4*, 290).

7. Karl Reinhardt too knows her name. See the note on p. 327 of his "Nietzsches Klage der Ariadne," at about mid-page.

8. See "The Convalescent," *4*, 272; see also M. Heidegger, *Nietzsche*, I, 307–10; English translation, Volume II, section 8.

9. Ironically, the pages from which Pana vanishes are riddled with a recurrent refrain: *Das Weib im Weibe erlösen*, or *freigeben*: redeem, or release, or liberate the woman in woman (see *10*, 516, 519, 527, 599, 604). The last reference adds the following explanation: "And may woman crave man—but not the masculine." In a less equivocal form the refrain emerges in the text of *Thus Spoke Zarathustra*, Part III, "On the Attenuating Virtue" (*4*, 213–14): "There is not much that attests to the man here: they therefore make their women masculine. For only the one who is man enough will *redeem* in woman *the woman*." Nietzsche nowhere specifies what it would mean to be man enough, or over-man

enough. Enough. The possibilities of dissimulation and (self-) deception here are limitless. On Deleuze's use of "the Attenuating Virtue," see p. 30, above.

10. The *Nachlass* editors have not speculated on the meaning of the number 30 after each phrase of the plan.

11. Note that the above plan for Part IV originates in autumn, 1883, before Part III itself is composed. Hence the plans for Part III go on.

12. See Bernard Pautrat, "Nietzsche médusé," in *Nietzsche aujourd'hui?* (Paris: UGE 10/18, 1973), I, 9–30. The final three pages of Pautrat's lecture would have to be rewritten in order to absorb an enormous range of distances and differences—some of them introduced by Rodolphe Gasché's versatile "Archiloque," *Nietzsche aujourd'hui?* I, 204–08.

Chapter Four: Calina

1. Reinhardt (332) is correct when he asserts that the poem "Venice," in which these words appear (see *Ecce Homo*, 6, 291), is thus much older, at least in inspiration, than interpreters have often claimed.

2. See Krell, "Female Parts in *Timaeus*," p. 401. Even the god Dionysos is so ravaged: Pentheus (*The Bacchae*, l.236) rebukes him for ὅσσοις χάριτας Ἀφροδίτης ἔχων, "having in his two eyes the ravishments of Aphrodite." On the "bitch sensuality," *die Hündin Sinnlichkeit*, see also *10*, 47: "The bitch sensuality, who craves a bite of flesh, knows how to beg very nicely for a bite of spirit." The original passage in the ms. of ASZ, crossed out at some stage, read (*14*, 666): "Sensuality comes around like a dog that wants a bite of flesh—even in the most intellectual kinds of comportment between the 2 sexes." In Eric Blondel's "Nietzsche: Life as Metaphor," an attempt is made to equate the body with "the father," murdered and repressed. But is not precisely this— the mother? See David B. Allison, ed., *The New Nietzsche: Contemporary Styles of Interpretation* (New York: Delta, 1977), pp. 154–56. Nor will it do to allow this note to end without observing that the bitch sensuality hounds the Hellenic-Hebraic-Christian tradition from beginning to end, from Genesis to Apocalypse, from Timaeus, Paul (*bonum est homini mulierem non tangere*), Tertullian (*mulier est templum super cloacam*), and Augustine (*tenaciter alligabar ex femina*) to the famous case of Jean-Jacques—as discussed by Derrida, *De la grammatologie* (Paris: Minuit, 1967), pp. 207–26. To such an extent that one is tempted to believe that the entire history of writing and reading hinges and unhinges on the question of sensuality, death, and woman.

3. The word *Entsprungen* encapsulates the entire ambiguity: "leapt away from" myself, but also "descended from" or "engendered by" myself.

4. See the famous Jules Bonnet photograph of Paul Rée, Nietzsche, and Lou (taken in Lucerne during May of 1882), discussed by Janz at II, 130. R. Hinton Thomas discusses Nietzsche's "whip" in the Appendix to his *Nietzsche in German Politics and Society, 1890–1918* (Manchester: Manchester University Press, 1983), pp. 132–40.

5. See p. 39 above. A far more earnest reading of "Daughters," but one that leaves out of account the doubling I wish to emphasize, may be found in C. A. Miller, "Nietzsche's 'Daughters of the Desert': A Reconsideration," in *Nietzsche-Studien*, Bd. 2 (1973), pp. 157–95. See esp. pp. 175–78, 183, and 190.

6. Ariadne's dream is reported at *10*, 433: "Dionysos on a tiger: the skull of a goat: a panther. Ariadne dreaming: 'Abandoned by the hero, I dream the over-hero.' To say nothing of Dionysos." See also *Thus Spoke Zarathustra*, Part II, "On the Sublime," which alludes throughout to the hero Theseus as the sublime one. At *4*, 152 we read: "For this is the secret of the soul: only when the hero has abandoned her does another approach her in dreams—the over-hero."

7. Although Nietzsche most often takes the part of Dionysos, to have the laugh of Ariadne, this is not always the case. The shameless god is not always Nietzsche's peer. In the following note, from the years 1885–86 (*12*, 76 and 178), the narrator resembles Ariadne more than anyone else—an Ariadne not yet sardonic, not yet the doom of heroes:

> "It seems to me you have something vicious up your sleeve," I once said to the god Dionysos; "namely, you plan to destroy the human race?" —"Perhaps," replied the god. "But only in order to get something out of it." —"What?" I asked, being curious. —"'Who?' is the proper question," retorted Dionysos. He then grew taciturn, in a way that is peculiar to him, that is, seductively. —You should have seen him! It was spring, and all the wood was bursting with the vigor of youth.

8. As Pierre Klossowski has done, with great sensitivity. See the final three sections of *Nietzsche et le cercle vicieux* (Paris: Mercure de France, 1969), pp. 251–367, "Consultation with the Paternal Shadow," "The Convalescent's Loveliest Invention," and "Euphoria in Turin."

Appendix: The Principal German Texts

1. *Die Käfer* may actually be beetles or lady-bugs; but I am supposing they are "young girls," "pretty little things."

2. An alternative translation: ". . . and, dissolving science, he turns it against itself." The *sich selbst* is difficult to interpret. Geneviève Bianquis, in F. Nietzsche, *La naissance de la philosophie à l'époche de la tragédie grecque* (Paris: Gallimard, 1938), p. 150, reads: ". . . abolissant la science et se condamnant lui-même."

3. Note the masculine form ("Ein Freund"), surprising in the present context.

4. Because of their central importance for my own work, all eight fragments, at 7, 233–37, should be examined. Here I reproduce only those portions cited in my text.

5. *Gegen* may of course mean either that Corinna walks *toward* Empedocles or that she now *opposes* him. Cf. "Dionysos gegen den Gekreuzigten. . . ."

6. Underscored several times—and utterly baffling!

7. The word *ihre* is difficult to interpret in the absence of any context: it may mean "their" soul and skin, if these be collective nouns; "your" is unlikely, because of both the lower-case i and the familiar form *euch* below. I therefore read it as "her" soul, "her" skin. But whose, hers?

8. The plan appears here unabridged, whereas in my text a number of sentences have been deleted.

9. Perhaps the best commentary on this equivocal exclamation is the fragment cited on p. 65, above: 16 [8] 1883; *10*, 500.

10. Is it already clear to Nietzsche by the autumn of 1887 what form this *Klage* will take? Has he already an eye and ear on the "Magician's Song"? And is the Ariadne of this *Satyrspiel* one who *could* lament? "Ich bin meines Mitleidens müde. . . ."

INDEX